Evaluating Administrative Services and Programs

Jon F. Wergin, *Editor*
Virginia Commonwealth University

Larry A. Braskamp, *Editor*
University of Illinois, Urbana–Champaign

NEW DIRECTIONS FOR INSTITUTIONAL RESEARCH
PATRICK T. TERENZINI, *Editor-in-Chief*
University of Georgia

MARVIN W. PETERSON, *Associate Editor*
University of Michigan

Number 56, Winter 1987

Paperback sourcebooks in
The Jossey-Bass Higher Education Series

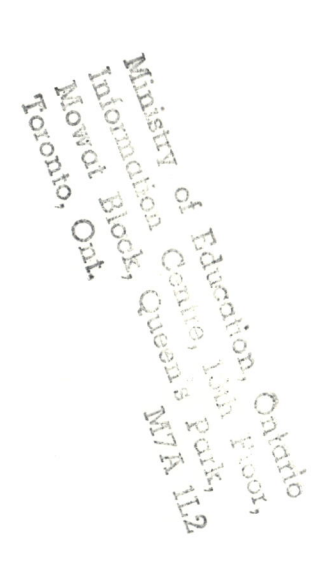

Jossey-Bass Inc., Publishers
San Francisco • London

Jon F. Wergin, Larry A. Braskamp (eds.).
Evaluating Administrative Services and Programs.
New Directions for Institutional Research, no. 56.
Volume XIV, Number 4.
San Francisco: Jossey-Bass, 1987.

New Directions for Institutional Research
Patrick T. Terenzini, *Editor-in-Chief*
Marvin W. Peterson, *Associate Editor*

Copyright © 1987 by Jossey-Bass Inc., Publishers
and
Jossey-Bass Limited

Copyright under International, Pan American, and Universal Copyright Conventions. All rights reserved. No part of this issue may be reproduced in any form—except for brief quotation (not to exceed 500 words) in a review or professional work—without permission in writing from the publishers.

New Directions for Institutional Research is published quarterly by Jossey-Bass Inc., Publishers (publication number USPS 098-830), and is sponsored by the Association for Institutional Research. The volume and issue numbers above are included for the convenience of libraries. Second-class postage paid at San Francisco, California, and at additional mailing offices. POSTMASTER: Send address changes to Jossey-Bass Inc., Publishers, 433 California Street, San Francisco, California 94104.

Editorial correspondence should be sent to the Editor-in-Chief, Patrick T. Terenzini, Institute of Higher Education, University of Georgia, Athens, Georgia 30602.

Library of Congress Catalog Card Number LC 85-645339
International Standard Serial Number ISSN 0271-0579
International Standard Book Number ISBN 1-55542-946-7

Cover art by WILLI BAUM
Manufactured in the United States of America

Ordering Information

The paperback sourcebooks listed below are published quarterly and can be ordered either by subscription or single copy.

Subscriptions cost $48.00 per year for institutions, agencies, and libraries. Individuals can subscribe at the special rate of $36.00 per year *if payment is by personal check*. (Note that the full rate of $48.00 applies if payment is by institutional check, even if the subscription is designated for an individual.) Standing orders are accepted.

Single copies are available at $11.95 when payment accompanies order. (California, New Jersey, New York, and Washington, D.C., residents please include appropriate sales tax.) For billed orders, cost per copy is $11.95 plus postage and handling.

Substantial discounts are offered to organizations and individuals wishing to purchase bulk quantities of Jossey-Bass sourcebooks. Please inquire.

Please note that these prices are for the academic year 1987–88 and are subject to change without notice. Also, some titles may be out of print and therefore not available for sale.

To ensure correct and prompt delivery, all orders must give either the *name of an individual* or an *official purchase order number*. Please submit your order as follows:

Subscriptions: specify series and year subscription is to begin.
Single Copies: specify sourcebook code (such as, IR1) and first two words of title.

Mail orders for United States and Possessions, Latin America, Canada, Japan, Australia, and New Zealand to:
Jossey-Bass Inc., Publishers
433 California Street
San Francisco, California 94104

Mail orders for all other parts of the world to:
Jossey-Bass Limited
28 Banner Street
London EC1Y 8QE

New Directions for Institutional Research Series
Patrick T. Terenzini *Editor-in-Chief*
Marvin W. Peterson, *Associate Editor*

IR1   *Evaluating Institutions for Accountability,* Howard R. Bowen
IR2   *Assessing Faculty Effort,* James I. Doi
IR3   *Toward Affirmative Action,* Lucy W. Sells

IR4   *Organizing Nontraditional Study,* Samuel Baskin
IR5   *Evaluating Statewide Boards,* Robert O. Berdahl
IR6   *Assuring Academic Progress Without Growth,* Allan M. Cartter
IR7   *Responding to Changing Human Resource Needs,* Raul Heist, Jonathan R. Warren
IR8   *Measuring and Increasing Academic Productivity,* Robert A. Wallhaus
IR9   *Assessing Computer-Based System Models,* Thomas R. Mason
IR10 *Examining Departmental Management,* James Smart, James Montgomery
IR11 *Allocating Resources Among Departments,* Paul L. Dressel, Lou Anna Kimsey Simon
IR12 *Benefiting from Interinstitutional Research,* Marvin W. Peterson
IR13 *Applying Analytic Methods to Planning and Management,* David S. P. Hopkins, Roger G. Scroeder
IR14 *Protecting Individual Rights to Privacy in Higher Education,* Alton L. Taylor
IR15 *Appraising Information Needs of Decision Makers,* Carl R. Adams
IR16 *Increasing the Public Accountability of Higher Education,* John K. Folger
IR17 *Analyzing and Constructing Cost,* Meredith A. Gonyea
IR18 *Employing Part-Time Faculty,* David W. Leslie
IR19 *Using Goals in Research and Planning,* Robert Fenske
IR20 *Evaluating Faculty Performance and Vitality,* Wayne C. Kirschling
IR21 *Developing a Total Marketing Plan,* John A. Lucas
IR22 *Examining New Trends in Administrative Computing,* E. Michael Staman
IR23 *Professional Development for Institutional Research,* Robert G. Cope
IR24 *Planning Rational Retrenchment,* Alfred L. Cooke
IR25 *The Impact of Student Financial Aid on Institutions,* Joe B. Henry
IR26 *The Autonomy of Public Colleges,* Paul L. Dressel
IR27 *Academic Program Evaluation,* Eugene C. Craven
IR28 *Academic Planning for the 1980s,* Richard B. Heydinger
IR29 *Institutional Assessment for Self-Improvement,* Richard I. Miller
IR30 *Coping with Faculty Reduction,* Stephen R. Hample
IR31 *Evaluation of Management and Planning Systems,* Nick L. Poulton
IR32 *Increasing the Use of Institutional Research,* Jack Lindquist
IR33 *Effective Planned Change Strategies,* G. Melvin Hipps
IR34 *Qualitative Methods for Institutional Research,* Eileen Kuhns, S. V. Martorana
IR35 *Information Technology: Innovations and Applications,* Bernard Sheehan
IR36 *Studying Student Attrition,* Ernest T. Pascarella
IR37 *Using Research for Strategic Planning,* Norman P. Uhl
IR38 *The Politics and Pragmatics of Institutional Research,* James W. Firnberg, William F. Lasher
IR39 *Applying Methods and Techniques of Futures Research,* James L. Morrison, William L. Renfro, Wayne I. Boucher
IR40 *College Faculty: Versatile Human Resources in a Period of Constraint,* Roger G. Baldwin, Robert T. Blackburn
IR41 *Determining the Effectiveness of Campus Services,* Robert A. Scott
IR42 *Issues in Pricing Undergraduate Education,* Larry H. Litten
IR43 *Responding to New Realities in Funding,* Larry L. Leslie
IR44 *Using Microcomputers for Planning and Management Support,* William L. Tetlow
IR45 *Impact and Challenges of a Changing Federal Role,* Virginia Ann Hodgkinson

IR46 *Institutional Research in Transition,* Marvin W. Peterson, Mary Corcoran
IR47 *Assessing Educational Outcomes,* Peter T. Ewell
IR48 *The Use of Data in Discrimination Issues Cases,* William Rosenthal, Bernard Yancey
IR49 *Applying Decision Support Systems in Higher Education,* John Rohrbaugh, Anne Taylor McCartt
IR50 *Measuring Faculty Research Performance,* John W. Creswell
IR51 *Enhancing the Management of Fund Raising,* John A. Dunn, Jr.
IR52 *Environmental Scanning for Strategic Leadership,* Patrick M. Callan
IR53 *Conducting Interinstitutional Comparisons,* Paul T. Brinkman
IR54 *Designing and Using Market Research,* Robert S. Lay, Jean J. Endo
IR55 *Managing Information in Higher Education,* E. Michael Staman

The Association for Institutional Research was created in 1966 to benefit, assist, and advance research leading to improved understanding, planning, and operation of institutions of higher education. Publication policy is set by its Publications Board.

PUBLICATIONS BOARD
Penny A. Wallhaus (Chairperson), Northwestern University
Peter T. Ewell, National Center for Higher Education Management Systems (NCHEMS)
Judith D. Hackman, Yale University
Mantha Vlahos Mehallis, Nova University
John C. Smart, Virginia Polytechnic Institute and State University
Richard A. Voorhees, Arapahoe Community College

EX-OFFICIO MEMBERS OF THE PUBLICATIONS BOARD
Ann K. Dickey, Saginaw Valley State College
Patrick T. Terenzini, University of Georgia
John A. Lucas, William Rainey Harper College
Charles F. Elton, University of Kentucky

EDITORIAL ADVISORY BOARD
All members of the Publications Board and:
Frederick E. Balderston, University of California, Berkeley
Roberta D. Brown, Arkansas College
Lyman A. Glenny, University of California, Berkeley (retired)
David S. P. Hopkins, Stanford University
Roger G. Schroeder, University of Minnesota
Robert J. Silverman, Ohio State University
Martin A. Trow, University of California, Berkeley

For information about the Association for Institutional Research, write:

>AIR Executive Office
>314 Stone Building
>Florida State University
>Tallahassee, FL 32306

>(904) 644-4470

Contents

Editors' Notes 1
Jon F. Wergin, Larry A. Braskamp

1. A Perspective on Evaluating Administrative Units in Higher Education 3
Richard F. Wilson
The evaluation design employed depends on evaluation purposes, information sought, and characteristics of the unit evaluated.

2. Evaluating Institutional Planning 15
Robert C. Shirley
Focal points for evaluation of strategic and operational planning include decisions to be made, data to be examined, and processes to be employed.

3. Evaluating Business Affairs: Complexity Demands Multiple Criteria and Approaches 25
Alan T. Seagren, Gary A. Miller
Evaluation of business affairs offices should focus on cost, confidentiality, user satisfaction, and service availability.

4. Beyond Ws and Ls: Evaluating Intercollegiate Athletics Programs 37
Barbara Gross Davis
Athletics programs must develop competitive programs while maintaining institutional integrity.

5. Evaluating Student Support Services 49
William E. Sedlacek
Useful evaluations need to recognize the importance of nontraditional student outcome variables.

6. Evaluating Counseling Centers 59
Robert D. Brown
Evaluation must respect the varied purposes of counseling centers and focus on goals, activities, and impact measures.

7. Evaluating Faculty Development Programs: Program Goals First 71
Robert E. Young
Concerns about the effectiveness of faculty development programs must begin with a comprehensive assessment of their goals.

8. **Evaluating Campus Computing Services: Taming the Technology** 83
Robert G. Gillespie
The explosive growth of computer technologies requires development of a common framework for their evaluation.

9. **Evaluating Administrative Services and Programs: Making the Process More Useful** 93
Jon F. Wergin, Larry A. Braskamp
The ultimate purpose of all evaluation is to enhance institutional effectiveness.

Index 101

Editors' Notes

Much has been written in recent years about the status of higher education in America. Reports published by the National Institute of Education (1984), the National Endowment for the Humanities (Bennett, 1984), the Association of American Colleges (1985), and the Carnegie Foundation for the Advancement of Teaching (Boyer, 1987) call for substantial undergraduate curriculum reform and better methods for assessing outcomes of liberal learning. In contrast, little has been written about ways of assessing an institution's administrative programs and support services, programs that exist as resources for administrators, faculty, and students. Some of these programs, such as faculty development and academic support, are still seen by many faculty and administrators as experimental, while others, such as financial services and offices of long-range planning, have become permanent fixtures in the college structure. Together, these offices consume substantial time and resources. They also share a largely peripheral status within their academic organizations, even though their college's image and overall health are at least in part determined by their effectiveness.

The purpose of this volume is to present a perspective on how colleges and universities might assess their administrative and support programs. It differs from an earlier volume on this topic (Scott, 1984) in two ways. First, rather than focusing on a review of extant program evaluation models for their applicability, we have chosen a more pragmatic approach by discussing pertinent assessment issues and methods within the context of these programs themselves. Second, in this age of "information based" organizations (Drucker, 1985), responsibilities for evaluation have shifted from a reliance on external evaluations conducted by accrediting agencies or consultants to internal evaluations conducted within the organizations themselves as part of routine administrative practice. The central questions addressed here are: How can institutional researchers and academic administrators authorize and produce information about program effectiveness that is useful for decision making? and, How are administrators to know how well these administrative and support services and programs are working, and what might be done to improve them?

Organization of the Volume

In Chapter One, Wilson summarizes the range of available models and strategies for evaluation and suggests criteria by which administrators might set the scope and boundaries of evaluation projects. The other authors describe how assessment might be approached within the setting of a particular program or function. Each reviews important contextual factors, such as a program's stated or implied purpose, clients, and sources of financial or political support; suggested effectiveness criteria by which the program might be judged; and strategies for collecting and interpreting needed information. In our final chapter we consider the implications of the authors' ideas from the perspective of the institutional researcher or administrator: Why undertake formal evaluation at all? What are the important features an evaluation should have, given differing program contexts? and, How can evaluation lead to a campus that is more effective and vital?

In this volume we have attempted to strike a balance between the abstract and the concrete by looking at how evaluation is practiced in seven diverse institutional settings and what the commonalities and differences are among these settings. Our hope is that the volume will have a wider applicability beyond the programs and offices discussed here.

Jon F. Wergin
Larry A. Braskamp
Editors

References

Association of American Colleges. "Integrity in the College Curriculum." *Chronicle of Higher Education*, February 18, 1985, pp. 12-30.
Bennett, W. J. "To Reclaim a Legacy: Text of Report on Humanities in Education." *Chronicle of Higher Education*, November 28, 1984, pp. 16-21.
Boyer, E. *College: The Undergraduate Experience in America*. New York: Harper & Row, 1987.
Drucker, P. F. "Playing in the Information-Based Orchestra." *Wall Street Journal*, June 4, 1985, p. 32.
National Institute of Education. "Involvement in Learning: Realizing the Potential of American Higher Education." *Chronicle of Higher Education*, October 24, 1984, pp. 35-49.
Scott, R. A. (ed.). *Determining the Effectiveness of Campus Services*. New Directions for Institutional Research, no. 41. San Francisco: Jossey-Bass, 1984.

Jon F. Wergin is associate director of the Center for
Educational Development and Faculty Resources at Virginia
Commonwealth University in Richmond.

Larry A. Braskamp is director of instructional and
management services at the University of Illinois,
Urbana-Champaign.

The challenge in evaluating administrative units is to differentiate the designs on the basis of the characteristics of the units and the information being sought.

A Perspective on Evaluating Administrative Units in Higher Education

Richard F. Wilson

Over the past ten years much has been written about program evaluation in higher education. This attention has been stimulated by a desire to collect systematic information about program quality, to make wise decisions about resource allocation and reallocation, and to meet requirements and expectations of external constituencies. In almost all instances, however, these evaluations have been focused on academic programs; very few institutions have given more than passing attention to academic support and administrative units. At one level this attention is understandable; the mission of a college or university is not to "do administration" but to provide instruction, research, or service. It therefore follows that initial interest in program evaluation would focus on the activities emanating from these missions. However, there are some other reasons why administrative units have been neglected.

There is a perception that the performance of many administrative units is more easily assessed than is the performance of academic units. In a very general sense, it is easier to determine whether the development office is doing a good job of fund raising than it is to assess whether a department is providing good instruction. In addition, because the staff of most administrative units do not have tenure, there is a presumption that those who are performing poorly will be replaced.

Part of the reluctance to evaluate administrative units stems from the fact that many units are quite small, often no larger than an institution's smallest academic department. Consequently, there is a feeling that a formal evaluation of such units is hardly worth the effort.

Finally, administrative units have not been evaluated because every unit requires a unique evaluation plan. Each evaluation requires considerable time to identify appropriate performance measures and establish data collection procedures for the unit being evaluated. There is greater functional similarity across academic units than across administrative units. The functional uniqueness of each administrative unit has been a significant impediment to evaluating these units.

Renewed Interest

Although the conditions described above still exist, a few institutions have begun to give serious attention to evaluating the performance of administrative units. There are several reasons for this movement. First, many institutions now have a reasonably well-defined process for evaluating academic units. Barak (1982) found that 82 percent of the institutions in his national study had some kind of evaluation process for academic programs. With that process in place, institutions have turned their attention to the performance of the rest of the organization.

Faculty have also been responsible for some of the movement to evaluate administrative units. Such evaluations have become more of a concern to faculty as the size of administrative units has grown. Their concern about the performance of what appears to be a mushrooming administrative structure on many campuses is justified. Individually, most administrative units require a small portion of an institution's budget; but together, their total expenditure is sufficient to justify close attention. In a few states (for example, Illinois), state coordinating boards have begun to require that administrative units be evaluated.

This combination of factors has led many institutions to give serious thought to ways of evaluating administrative units. The difficulty is how to organize a process that will be equally useful in evaluating, for example, an office of admissions and records and a campus police force.

General Context

Although administrative units have some unique characteristics that require special attention in an evaluation, a number of general design issues and evaluation principles have been studied extensively and have relevance to the evaluation of administrative units. The steps to be

followed in developing an evaluation plan do not change. Barak (1982) has identified the following ten steps for which planning must occur:
- Identify evaluation purposes
- Conceptualize the process
- Develop consensus
- Select reviewers
- Collect data
- Assess the data
- Conduct the evaluation
- Develop recommendations
- Implement and use the results
- Evaluate the review process.

The first two steps on this list are especially important and will be discussed below.

Identify Evaluation Purposes. There usually are a variety of reasons for developing an evaluation process, and it is important to clarify what these reasons are and to make sure they are compatible. Evaluations may be requested in order to improve program performance, assess efficiency, satisfy external accountability requirements, or increase productivity. Essentially, the question is, What is to be accomplished through evaluation? A clear statement of purposes is necessary as a guide to those establishing evaluation procedures and to those making evaluative judgments.

Conceptualize the Process. A number of models have been proposed for evaluating programs. These models may be grouped into one of the following general categories: (1) goal-based, (2) responsive, (3) decision-oriented, and (4) connoisseurship (Conrad and Wilson, 1985). The goal-based model requires that goals and objectives be specified, standards of acceptable performance be identified for each goal, data be collected that reflect the standards, and judgments be made about whether the standards have been met (Tyler, 1949).

The responsive model pays little attention to formal program goals, focusing instead on the issues and concerns of those who are involved or interested in a program. Attention is given to program activities, regardless of what the goals might be (Stake, 1975). In the decision-oriented model, an evaluation seeks to respond to the information needs of those who have questions about a program. The objective of these evaluations is to collect information that will enable wise decisions to be made (Stufflebeam and others, 1971).

Finally, the connoisseurship model relies upon the expertise and insight of an expert in the field. The typical form of this model is the peer review. Data may be collected from a variety of sources, but the knowledge and experience of the expert forms the basis for evaluative judgments (Eisner, 1975).

Most institutions do not implement a pure form of any of these models, preferring instead to incorporate components from each one. Nevertheless, an evaluation plan will have a predominant orientation toward one of the models identified above, and it is important to be clear about the assumptions and implications of that model.

General Principles

Experience with evaluations in other settings suggests that several principles should be embodied in any evaluation. The one at the top of the list is fairness. The fairness of what is being done should be reviewed at every stage of the process. The importance of conducting an evaluation that is fair is easy to affirm but sometimes is difficult to uphold as an evaluation unfolds. An evaluation that cannot be attacked on substantive grounds will become easy prey if the procedures used are perceived as unfair.

Another important principle is timeliness. Every evaluation will require some trade-offs between the ideal and the acceptable design. The development of a plan that will satisfy the information needs of those requesting the evaluation is not too difficult; the problem is whether the design that is proposed can be completed with the resources available (staff and budget) and within the time period necessary for the results to be used. It is more important to complete a good evaluation on time than an excellent one late.

An evaluation also should be responsive, that is, sensitive to the context and climate in which the evaluation will occur. This can be accomplished when there are adequate resources and some expectation that the results of reviews will be used to enhance existing programs and activities. More frequently, however, evaluations are undertaken because an institution faces serious budget or enrollment problems and is looking for ways to reduce commitments and reallocate resources. In this climate there is greater interest by internal and external constituencies, and each step in the process will be debated at length. An institution may have a standard evaluation plan, but increased surveillance by interested parties makes it highly unlikely that standard evaluations will be implemented.

Every evaluation should provide for frequent interaction between the evaluators and those being evaluated so that they can determine ways to make evaluation results relevant and useful. This is especially important for units with a "boundary-spanning" mission, one that includes constituencies inside and outside the institution. Examples include offices concerned with alumni affairs, public affairs, and development. Soliciting the views of external constituencies will require extra time and effort. Nevertheless, the credibility of an evaluation depends on the evaluators' willingness to adapt standard procedures to unique circumstances.

Special Considerations

Although the evaluation of administrative units is similar in many ways to other types of evaluations, some special circumstances must be considered. In contrast to the standard procedures that most institutions have developed to evaluate academic units, administrative units are so varied that standard procedures are useless. A general framework can be developed, but it is futile to spend time developing standards and measures that might be used for every evaluation. The basis on which performance is to be judged and the data are to be collected will vary from one unit to the next.

The establishment of comparison groups for administrative units is very difficult. Academic departments can be compared on, for example, teaching loads, if the teaching mode is similar for the departments. Similar cross-campus comparisons for administrative units are almost impossible. Therefore, data must be sought from units with the same mission at other institutions or advice sought from outside experts.

Given the lack of standards for evaluating administrative units, the use of outside experts can be quite helpful in assessing a unit's performance. The perspective of these experts may also prove valuable in addressing contentious issues and may add legitimacy to the review process, at least in the eyes of those being evaluated. The key is to identify in advance those questions that outside experts are in a position to answer. Without such planning, the report of an outside review team may document only what is already known.

The number of administrative units on many campuses will preclude a comprehensive evaluation, which requires considerable time, effort, and resources, of every unit. Even on a four- or five-year cycle, a detailed assessment of more than three or four administrative units each year may prove too burdensome. Griffin and Burks (1976) developed a comprehensive plan for evaluating administrative units within the University of California system. The plan was implemented but abandoned in a short time because the procedure was too complex.

For this reason, an institution may want to develop an evaluation scheme that allows cursory attention to be given to units that appear to be functioning well, thus reserving greater time for units where problems appear to exist or where concerns have been expressed. Alternatively, evaluations must be scheduled only on a selective basis.

Although faculty have helped stimulate the current interest in evaluating administrative units, in general they will not be enthusiastic about participating as reviewers of such units. In most instances, the work of administrative offices will be considered too far removed from the faculty member's area of expertise. Faculty members will not give such evaluations a high priority in terms of use of their time. This is not to suggest that the faculty will not participate, nor that they do not have something to contribute; they simply will be more interested in having the administrative units reviewed than in playing a lead role in the review process themselves.

A Framework for Evaluation

In 1981 a decision was made at the University of Illinois at Urbana–Champaign (UIUC) to begin evaluating administrative units. A planning committee was appointed to develop a procedure. The discussion that follows is drawn largely from the report of that committee (Wilson, McManus, and Todd, 1982) and from the experience of implementing the recommendations in the report.

The decision to evaluate administrative units was precipitated by two events: (1) a request from the Illinois Board of Higher Education to evaluate nonacademic and administrative units in colleges and universities in the state and (2) a resolution from the UIUC Senate asking the administration to develop criteria for evaluating the efficiency of administrative units. This resolution stemmed, in part, from a faculty interest in balancing a long-standing evaluation process for academic units with one that focused on administrative units.

A key principle that permeated discussions about the new evaluation process was that it should complement, not compete with, existing managerial practices. This principle led to the decision to decentralize the review process rather than to develop the capacity to evaluate all campus units centrally. Each vice-chancellor was given the responsibility of evaluating administrative units. The virtue of this arrangement was that the evaluation function was aligned with the budget and planning functions. Since the vice-chancellors were already responsible for the budgets for units in their areas, it made sense to involve them in the evaluation of those units. If changes were necessary, or if additional resources were needed, the vice-chancellors were in a position to respond.

Another reason to decentralize was the lack of enthusiasm for creating an evaluation office with campus-wide responsibilities and the scarcity of resources for such an effort. There also was some fear that a centralized office might, over time, establish an agenda that was not consistent with the needs of the campus. The general consensus was that this new evaluation responsibility could be assumed by someone already on the staffs of the vice-chancellors. This also would help ensure that the vice-chancellors were involved. The likelihood that the evaluations would be used was believed to be enhanced if the vice-chancellors gave this assignment to an immediate staff member.

The limitations of this approach are that evaluation expertise may or may not be a skill of the person assigned the task. Thus, some time may be lost while these skills are developed. Further, if evaluation is an added-on responsibility, the number of evaluations conducted would be limited. Finally, the decentralized approach makes it difficult for a campus-wide perspective to be invoked. One vice-chancellor may find a unit's performance to be completely satisfactory, while another may have serious concern.

These limitations influenced the way in which the evaluation process was designed at UIUC. The plan that was implemented offered four alternatives for evaluating administrative units: (1) desk review, (2) strategic review, (3) lateral review, and (4) comprehensive review. These alternatives provided considerable flexibility in the methodology followed and allowed the evaluation process to respond to a range of expectations.

Any institution that establishes a systematic evaluation process for all programs will find a program that is widely believed to be functioning well and in need of no major changes. The directors of such units monitor services carefully and can demonstrate that services are being provided in an efficient and effective way. Those to whom the unit reports will have few questions that an evaluation might answer and will have even fewer concerns about the unit. The unit may be willing to participate in an evaluation but might contend that little is to be gained from such an exercise. Excusing the unit from the review may create problems if there is an evaluation mandate from internal or external sources; establishing baseline information for subsequent evaluations is also imperiled. Such action may call into question the credibility of the evaluation process since it will not be clear to everyone why certain units do not have to be evaluated. For these reasons, evaluating all units is encouraged; the challenge is to differentiate the evaluations on the basis of the information that is desired.

Desk Review. In a desk review, a unit is asked to respond to a set of fundamental questions. This standard set of questions needs to be edited to make them relevant to the unit being evaluated or to address any special concerns. A few examples of the questions in this standard set are listed below:

1. What are the current objectives of the unit and the services being provided? What evidence exists to justify the need for these services? What services are needed that are not being provided?

2. What has been the budget for the unit as a whole and for each functional area over the past five years? How adequate is the present budget?

3. What statistical data exist on the annual services provided by the unit? How and when are services evaluated internally, and what standards are used to judge performance?

4. What are the major problems and constraints faced by the unit?

Once the questions to be included in the desk review are agreed on, the unit prepares a written response and submits it to the appropriate executive officer, who reviews the response and discusses it with the unit director. This conversation may conclude the evaluation or may lead to specific follow-up activities. The virtue of this approach is that program evaluation expectations have been met, but the level of effort has been matched to the perceived need. Desk reviews are relatively painless, unobtrusive, and inexpensive and usually can be completed in two or three months. However, such reviews may not prove very satisfactory if there are constituencies outside the unit that have concerns about the unit's performance. A desk review is not a very good way to ensure that a need for improvement is incorporated into an evaluation.

Strategic Review. The main difference between a strategic review and a desk review is that in a strategic review a small number of special concerns are singled out for attention. The unit being evaluated responds to the standard set of desk review questions but, in addition, is asked to address some specific questions or concerns that are of interest to those to whom the unit reports. Reviews of this type are reserved for units that appear to be functioning well generally but may have a few areas of special concern.

A typical approach to a strategic review would be for the unit under evaluation to respond to a standard questionnaire and for a committee to be appointed to study the special issues or concerns. The committee may consist of faculty or staff from the campus or peers in similar units from other institutions. The exact composition will depend upon the issue being explored.

A few years ago, the Office of Instructional Resources at UIUC was evaluated. The office prepared a response to a set of questions that had been developed on the basis of a standard questionnaire used in desk reviews. In addition, there was considerable interest in knowing how the faculty assessed the value and quality of services provided by the office. A survey was developed for this purpose and was augmented with a telephone interview of a random group of faculty members. In this way the evaluation satisfied the normal expectations and also addressed a question of strategic interest.

A strategic review is not envisioned to be a detailed assessment of a unit; the general idea is to conduct an evaluation that is somewhere between a desk review and a comprehensive evaluation. Given the attention to a specific set of questions or concerns, this type of review is modeled after the decision-oriented approach to evaluation.

Lateral Review. This type of review is not so much a specific methodology as a focus. On many campuses, certain support functions are carried out in more than one office. Thus, it frequently makes sense to conduct an evaluation that corresponds with functional rather than organizational structure. Activities such as placement, advising, and computer support are examples of functions assigned to more than one unit on a campus and thus are good candidates for lateral reviews. A lateral review may follow the guidelines for strategic or comprehensive evaluations.

Comprehensive Review. A comprehensive evaluation is reserved for those occasions in which a thorough review of an administrative unit is warranted. Such reviews may occur at the time of a change in leadership or when a definitive statement about a unit's efficiency or effectiveness is needed.

A good example of a comprehensive system for evaluating administrative units was developed at the University of Calgary. That system involved: (1) completion of a detailed self-study questionnaire by the unit under review, (2) appointment of an outside review team to study the unit and to prepare a report, and (3) development of a final report by a campus committee incorporating the unit's self-study, the outside reviewers' findings, and the committee members' own perceptions about the unit's performance in relation to campus expectations (Braun, 1982).

A comprehensive evaluation system allows multiple perspectives to be introduced into the evaluation process—from the unit, peers, and the campus. The chief disadvantage is that organizing an evaluation around these three components requires more time and resources than most institutions can commit on a regular basis. Both the University of Calgary system and the University of California system (mentioned earlier) appear to have failed, at least in part, because of their complexity.

Impact

The issue debated most frequently by those engaged in evaluation is whether such activities have any impact, that is, whether evaluations are used once they are completed. It is not easy to answer this question because recommendations may be implemented over a relatively long period of time, include subtle changes that are difficult to observe, provide leverage for action not envisioned in the evaluation report, and often confirm impressions that no change is required. In spite of these difficulties, it is important to monitor use of evaluation results.

A procedure for evaluating administrative units has been in place for five years at UIUC. There has not been a systematic assessment of the process, but several observations can be made. Approximately ten administrative units have been evaluated annually. In only one or two cases each year has something other than a desk review been conducted. On the one hand, this may validate the approach developed for these evaluations—that is, the nature of the review has been matched to the level of need. On the other hand, the preponderant use of desk reviews may mean that the process is not taken very seriously. In some instances, desk reviews are implemented because they satisfy the Board of Higher Education requirement that an evaluation be conducted.

However, some visible changes have occurred as a result of the evaluation process. Some support units have found the information collected as part of the desk reviews so informative that similar information is now collected on a regular basis. Several unit heads have commented on the desirability of retaining the evaluation process for no other reason than to provide an opportunity to bring the accomplishments as well as the needs of their units to the attention of campus administrators. Finally, in those instances in which strategic reviews have been implemented (one or two per year), action has been taken on recommendations emanating from specific questions. It is difficult, however, to attribute the actions solely to the evaluations; there usually have been several contributing factors.

The reason that a process for evaluating administrative units was instituted at UIUC stemmed from both institutional and state agency interests. The process has been satisfactory in meeting evaluation requirements of the Illinois Board of Higher Education. Although there is scattered evidence of use of evaluation results on campus, the process needs to be carefully reviewed before it can be stated that the evaluations have contributed significantly to unit efficiency and effectiveness.

References

Barak, R. J. *Program Review in Higher Education: Within and Without.* Boulder, Colo.: National Center for Higher Education Management Systems, 1982.

Braun, S. "Management Reviews: Assessing the Performance of Support Services in an Academic Environment." Paper presented at the annual meeting of the Association for Institutional Research, Denver, Colo., May 1982.

Conrad, C. F., and Wilson, R. F. *Academic Program Reviews.* ASHE-ERIC Higher Education Research Report, no. 5. Washington, D.C.: Association for the Study of Higher Education, 1985.

Eisner, E. W. *The Perceptive Eye: Toward the Reformation of Educational Evaluation.* Stanford, Calif.: Stanford Evaluation Consortium, 1975.

Griffin, G., and Burks, D. R. *Appraising Administrative Operations: Guide for Universities and Colleges.* Berkeley: University of California Systemwide Administration, 1976.

Stake, R. E. (ed.). *Evaluating the Arts in Education: A Responsive Approach.* Westerville, Ohio: Merrill, 1975.

Stufflebeam, D. L., Foley, W. J., Gephart, W. J., Guba, E. G., Hammond, R. L., Merriman, R. L., and Provus, M. M. *Educational Evaluation and Decision Making.* Itasca, Ill.: Peacock, 1971.

Tyler, R. W. *Basic Principles of Curriculum and Instruction: Syllabus for Education 360.* Chicago: University of Chicago Press, 1949.

Wilson, R. F., McManus, J. B., and Todd, R. K. *An Evaluation Plan for Administrative Units at the University of Illinois at Urbana-Champaign.* Champaign: University of Illinois, 1982.

Richard F. Wilson is associate chancellor at the University of Illinois at Urbana-Champaign, where he is principally responsible for campus planning activities. He formerly directed the department review program for the UIUC campus.

The planning effort must be assessed periodically to determine if the process and data employed are leading to effective decisions.

Evaluating Institutional Planning

Robert C. Shirley

Although approaches to planning vary dramatically from one institution of higher learning to another, most now recognize the need for systematic planning, that is, the articulation of goals, priorities, and actions to be pursued by the institution. Those institutions embarking on formal planning typically incorporate evaluation of one kind or another, particularly when trying to gauge the strengths and weaknesses of academic programs and administrative support activities. What is often lacking, however, is an evaluation of the planning function itself. This chapter suggests ways by which the planning function can be evaluated to determine if it is serving the best interests of the institution.

This chapter focuses first on the essential components of a planning process: the decisions to be made, the analytical focal points, and key process considerations. These components will be examined from both the institution's and individual units' perspectives in order to establish an overall framework for evaluation; thereafter, the chapter presents specific criteria for evaluating the planning effort.

Planning Defined

Although planning has been defined in various ways, most students of the subject now distinguish between strategic and operational planning (Ansoff, 1984; Wheelen and Hunger, 1984). At the institutional level, typical strategic planning focuses ultimately on determining mission and goals, target audiences, program priorities, geographic service area, comparative advantage, and specific objectives to be pursued as the institution moves through a defined time period (Lelong and Shirley, 1984). Strategic decisions made at the institutional level are frequently supported by analyses of the (1) external environment, (2) strengths and weaknesses of the enterprise, and (3) values of organizational members and other "stakeholders" (Christensen, Berg, and Salter, 1980, p. 11). The process employed to collect and analyze data and to reach closure on strategic issues takes various forms, usually depending on the degree of participation sought throughout the institution. In a normative sense, strategic planning at the unit level follows much the same pattern: A process is formed to ensure that the necessary data are examined and that strategic decisions complement the strategies being pursued at the institutional level appropriately (albeit often ambiguously).

Thus strategic planning focuses on answering the "what" questions faced by the institution and its individual units. By contrast, operational planning focuses on the "how" questions. Once strategies are established for the total institution, numerous operational considerations related to finances, facilities, enrollments, human resources, and organization must be addressed. At the institutional level, operational plans for these crucial areas also require that data be examined and decisions be made within a well-defined process to be successful. At the individual unit level, analogous operational decisions must be made if the unit's own strategic plan is to be successful.

In short, every institution and its individual units are faced with both strategic and operational decisions to answer the "what" and "how" questions, respectively. Moreover, these decisions must be supported by appropriate data and analyses to prevent undue reliance on intuition and impulse. Finally, a well-defined process must be developed to ensure that data and decisions are examined in the proper sequence and by the proper parties: decisions to be made, data to be examined, and process to be employed. These generic elements become, in turn, the focal points for evaluating both strategic and operational planning. The remainder of this chapter identifies the appropriate criteria for evaluating planning decisions, data, and process.

Criteria for Evaluating the Decisional Aspect of Planning

Strategic and operational planning processes must culminate in decisions about what the institution is seeking to accomplish and how the overall strategy will be implemented. The following criteria should be examined to determine if appropriate decisions have emerged from the planning process:

1. *Are the strategic directions of the institution clear and identifiable in words and in practice?* Without clarity of outcome objectives, of course, the ultimate goal of planning will not be realized. This criterion requires specificity about mission, goals, target audiences, program priorities, geographic service area, comparative advantage, and objectives of the institution—in short, its strategic profile. The criterion also refers to clarity in operational planning as well, particularly with regard to the plans for facilities, organization, finances, enrollments, and human resource development. The objective is to ensure that organizational members and external constituents understand the directions established for the future, even though no individual is likely to agree with every facet of the plan.

2. *Do the decisions contained in the plan represent a coherent course of action for the institution?* According to one definition, *coherence* requires "systematic connection, especially in logical discourse." The structure of decisions presented in a plan should display systematic connections and internal consistency; for example, the facilities plan (an operational decision) should be based on the academic program priorities of the institution (a strategic decision).

3. *Do the decisions take proper cognizance of trends outside the institution, internal strengths and weaknesses, and key personal and organizational values?* This criterion focuses on examining strategic decisions at the institutional and unit level in light of the directions suggested by the supporting analyses performed in the planning process. This is not to suggest that one must always follow the dictates of data and trends; however, one should be able to explain why a contrary direction was chosen. A great deal of ambiguity occurs when attempting to define the decisional implications of a given analysis. Thus, one should allow for judgment in the evaluation process as well as in the decisions themselves.

4. *Are there evidences that the decisions made as a result of planning are being implemented appropriately throughout the enterprise?* The plan must be implemented to be successful, and success depends ultimately on behavioral change throughout the institution. One must develop means for gauging the degree of consistency between the decisions themselves and the day-to-day behavior of individual members of the institution. Without such an evaluation, one cannot determine whether the strategic and operational plans for the institution have been internalized by those responsible for implementation.

5. *Are the decisions timely and reflective of the institutional life cycle?* The timeliness criterion requires a qualitative assessment of the degree of maturity of an institution, the external opportunities and threats that must be considered (such as funding changes by legislation, demographic changes, economic fluctuation, Affirmative Action regulations, and so on), and the resource base available. Institutions frequently aspire to goals that are simply unattainable in a given time period

because of lack of readiness for change, negative environmental conditions, or lack of resources. On the other hand, there are some institutions who under-aspire, failing to recognize the need and readiness for internal change, the very positive nature of some trends, and the quality and capability of the resource base—human, financial, and physical. In short, decisions made as a result of planning must be realistic and timely and fit the institutional life cycle properly.

These five critical questions evaluate the decisional aspects of planning, both strategic and operational. If decisions made as a result of planning display these attributes—clarity, coherence, analytical support, degree of implementation, and timeliness—then the chances for success are greatly enhanced.

Criteria for Evaluating Data Used in Planning

The following questions should be asked when examining the data employed for decision making.

1. *Are the data relevant to the decisional issues facing the institution?* This criterion constitutes the cornerstone of evaluation when examining the data employed in planning. Far too many planning processes are complicated unnecessarily by the collection of excessive and irrelevant data. When decisions are being made about the future, one naturally encounters a great deal of ambiguity. The reaction to such ambiguity often is excessive reliance on projections and other seemingly objective inputs designed to eliminate the ambiguities. Relevance to the issue at hand is often forgotten in such circumstances. It is far better to capture the essential and most relevant data. When examining data to determine relevance, one must always examine their degree of connection to the strategic and operational issues in the planning process.

2. *Has the appropriate quantity of data been employed in the decision-making process?* As implied by the preceding criterion, one can collect too much data if relevance is not carefully considered. On the other hand, one can just as easily use too little data in decision making. To determine if one has reached an appropriate balance between the two extremes, it is often useful to examine the data employed in planning after the plan has been fully developed. Whether too much or too little data were employed can be determined by interviews with participants in the process and by examining whether or not selected analyses were actually used for decisional purposes.

3. *Are the data sources of high quality?* Issues of quantity and relevance are extremely important, but one must also carefully assess the quality of the data sources utilized in planning. There are external and internal dimensions to this criterion. On the internal dimension, we must gauge the accuracy and timeliness of the data base employed, particularly as it relates to assessment of the strengths and weaknesses of the financial,

human, and physical resource base of the institution. On the external dimension, the secondary sources of data should be highly reliable. When one is faced with ambiguous issues, one tends to collect as much data as possible in order to shed light on the issues. The rush to accumulate data should be tempered by recognizing that studies from external sources differ greatly in quality of research design and methodology. It is helpful to have a person trained in research methods make judgments concerning quality of the data.

In summary, the three focal points for evaluating the data employed in planning are relevance, quantity, and quality. Such evaluation is often best conducted after initial planning decisions have been produced. Mistakes made during the initial stages of planning can then be corrected for subsequent rounds of planning decisions.

Criteria for Evaluating the Process

The following questions should be asked when evaluating the process employed for planning:

1. *Is there evidence of top management support for the planning effort?* Implied in this criterion is real and assertive support of planning, not merely lip service. With the increasing credibility of strategic planning, there is a tendency to "marshall the forces" and put in place a process for planning without realizing the commitment required. Most importantly, the upper echelons of administrative and faculty leadership must be committed to decision making as a result of planning, and especially to making hard choices among alternative goals, priorities, and future programs. Without such top-level support from the outset, the planning effort is doomed to failure (Thompson and Strickland, 1984). Moreover, such support must be evidenced throughout the process, particularly when critical and sensitive issues are being discussed. Without such commitment, particularly from the president, faculty and staff alike soon believe that little value is placed on closure and clarity.

2. *Have appropriate constituents been meaningfully involved in the planning process?* The word "meaningfully" is essential to this criterion, as it requires open and honest participation by affected parties (Brown and Moberg, 1980). Without meaningful involvement, it is impossible to achieve ownership of the decisions being made as a result of planning. Unanimity is not implied here, nor even consensus. Unless participation is widespread and meaningful, however, disagreements will not be open and straightforward. Thus, the purpose of meaningful participation is not to gain widespread agreement, although such convergence of views is always welcome. Rather, the purpose is to ensure a broad and diverse set of inputs and to ensure that most parties identify with the process, if not with the outcome.

3. *Does the process concentrate on substance rather than form?* As

the field of planning has evolved, so too have the jargon and trappings normally associated with evolution of a profession or discipline. In many instances, this has resulted in the design of a complex process that leads to little other than bureaucratic nicety. A classic example is not only asking common questions of all planning units at an institution but also requiring that those units respond in a common format. Asking common questions is important and appropriate, but insisting on a common format for response does little more than ease the task of the professional planning staff. In such circumstances, planning often becomes a simple exercise of filling out the forms, thereby diverting important energies and attitudes from the substantive issues that should be addressed.

Every institution needs to develop a conceptual framework for planning, a matrix or two (to contain environmental analysis, program review, and selected other issues), and a calendar of key target dates. Beyond these basic "forms," most institutions would be well-served by dispensing with much of the paperwork that has evolved in the past few years. If written institutional and unit strategic plans exceed fifteen to twenty pages, the focus on substance may be lost.

4. *Does the process provide for continuity?* Two dimensions are important here: continuity of the persons involved in planning and continuity from one planning cycle to the next. It is important that one person be charged with planning for overlaps among members of key planning groups so that continuity of perspective and institutional memory is achieved and with ensuring that the critical issues addressed in one planning cycle are properly influential during the next round of deliberations.

5. *Does the process culminate in decision making?* As previously indicated, decision making must be the point of closure during formal deliberations. Process is extremely important, but the process will be successful only to the extent that it produces meaningful decisions.

In summary, the key words in evaluation of process are *top management support, meaningful participation, concentration on substance rather than form, continuity,* and *decision-making results.* Many of these processes can be anticipated beforehand and planned for accordingly. Retrospective evaluation should be conducted, however, in order to ensure that the desired processes were fully achieved.

Methods of Evaluation

There are five responsible parties in the evaluation process—the governing board, president, planning council, planning support staff, and, for selected situations, a planning consultant—and their respective roles are explained below.

The governing board is ultimately responsible for the decisions emerging from the planning process, and thus the board's evaluation efforts should focus on these decisions. The board should have little concern for the evaluation criteria related to data and process, as these two areas represent the details of planning. In evaluating the decisional results, the board should focus on the five questions raised in this chapter, requiring as input to their deliberations a concise, annual report by the president addressing explicitly the five criteria. Based on this report and on direct examination of the written plan itself, the board should decide whether the planning process is producing the desired results.

The responsibility of the president in the evaluation process is twofold. First, he or she must provide input to the board as discussed above. Second, and most importantly, he or she must assume the primary responsibility for ensuring that the evaluation process is performed throughout the institution. The president must assign responsibility for evaluation and stress the importance of such efforts. Once responsibilities are assigned and timetables are set, the president's personal role in evaluation must focus on the five criteria related to decision making. He or she must ensure that planning support staff and others complete the evaluation of data and process in a timely manner and that appropriate correctional action is taken when necessary.

The planning council should approve the overall evaluation design, including types of information to be employed (for example, surveys of participants in the planning process, anecdotal evidences from colleagues, survey of community attitudes). The council should advise the president about whether the planning process is producing the desired results and serving the best interests of the institution. Such a council can also provide valuable input concerning the consensus for planning on campus, that is, some sense as to the credibility of the process throughout the institution. (Note: In certain types of situations, it is more appropriate to establish an ad hoc evaluation group, particularly if the planning process has resulted in highly controversial recommendations by the planning council.)

Planning support staff must play a primary role in the evaluation process, as it is this person or group to whom the president and planning council must turn for the evaluation design and for detailed studies when necessary. In addition to overall evaluation design, the planning staff's efforts will focus most importantly on the data employed and the attributes of the process. Support staff must initiate both the conceptual and methodological aspects of evaluation in order to properly support the planning council and the president. Once the president has determined that an evaluation effort is important and is to be implemented, the planning support staff must bear the responsibility for a successful effort.

Finally, in many instances it will be helpful to employ the services of a consultant. Such a person can bring a fresh, unbiased perspective to evaluating planning decisions, data, and process. Several institutions have found it economical and effective to employ the services of a consultant to evaluate their efforts annually and to improve the planning functions.

The methods of evaluation to be employed by the five parties will vary significantly, depending on the criteria being addressed. The evaluation of the decisions requires the most judgment, although perceptions of decisional results can be collected and quantified in appropriate instances. It may be helpful, for example, to conduct surveys both on campus and in the community to determine the degree of understanding of the institution's mission and priorities. If perceptions vary widely, then one may conclude that greater precision in both written and verbal communication is necessary to clarify the strategic directions of the institution.

The evaluation of planning data and process is, in a relative sense, easier to accomplish than the evaluation of decisions made. The planning support staff must take the lead with the planning council to examine the uses (and abuses) of data in a recently completed planning cycle. Post hoc evaluation efforts are most desirable in this case and should be conducted soon after the completion of a given annual cycle. The most common approach to evaluating data involves examination of the data actually used in relation to the issues addressed during the planning process. One generally finds a remarkable degree of consensus concerning the data that were helpful in decision making and those that were not. The same holds true for data sources, as one can readily gauge the degree of accuracy of data when examining past events or predictions.

The evaluation of the planning process in terms of the criteria discussed earlier is also reasonably straightforward. The most common method is to survey the participants' attitudes to determine perceptions concerning the support of top management, the degree of meaningful participation, whether the planning process focuses on substantive matters, and the extent to which the process produces meaningful decisions for the institution. The old proverb that "perceptions are everything" applies in this instance, as the ultimate goal is credibility of the process within the institution.

Summary

The principal challenge in evaluating the planning function lies in the organization of the process, not in the techniques to be employed. The thirteen questions presented in this chapter constitute the focal points of evaluation and apply equally to strategic and operational planning. The president must play the lead role in the planning effort and, consequently, in ensuring that an evaluation process is designed and implemented properly by planning support staff. Management of the evaluation process should be the primary responsibility of the planning support staff and the planning council of the institution. Survey research will be the most common method of evaluation and should involve primarily members of the campus community. For selected issues a community survey also may be desirable.

Finally, these thirteen questions should be asked at least annually when evaluating the institution's planning effort. As is the case with any evaluation mechanism, however, the criteria are most useful when used as guidelines for initiating a planning effort. The results of evaluation can then be used as feedback for revising the guidelines for subsequent planning cycles.

References

Ansoff, H. I. *Implementing Strategic Management.* Englewood Cliffs, N.J.: Prentice/Hall, 1984.
Brown, W. B., and Moberg, A. J. *Organization Theory and Management: A Macro Approach.* New York: Wiley, 1980.
Christensen, C. R., Berg, N. A., and Salter, M. S. *Policy Formulation and Administration.* Homewood, Ill.: Richard D. Irwin, 1980.
Lelong, D., and Shirley, R. "Planning: Identifying the Focal Points for Action." *Planning for Higher Education,* 1984, *12* (4), 1-7.
Thompson, A. A., Jr., and Strickland, A. J., III. *Strategic Management: Concepts and Cases.* Plano, Tex.: Business Publications, 1984.
Wheelen, T. L., and Hunger, J. D. *Strategic Management.* Reading, Mass.: Addison-Wesley, 1984.

Robert C. Shirley is president of the University of Southern Colorado. He has been a consultant in strategic planning to over seventy-five colleges and universities.

Alternative approaches are required to evaluate the effectiveness and efficiency of business affairs in higher education.

Evaluating Business Affairs: Complexity Demands Multiple Criteria and Approaches

Alan T. Seagren, Gary A. Miller

This chapter will focus on the evaluation of business affairs in colleges and universities. Although the term *business affairs* typically covers a wide range of activities and services, for the purposes of this chapter, *business affairs* will include four areas of management identified by Welzenbach (1982) and the administrative services related to them: *administrative management*: institutional planning, space management, management information systems, records management, risk management and insurance, fiscal administration sponsored programs, legal services, management of student financial aid funds, personnel administration and labor relations; *business management*: purchasing goods and services, auxiliary enterprises and other services, physical plant (planning, design, construction, operation, and maintenance), environmental health and safety, security and law enforcement, and transportation; *fiscal management*: administration of endowments and similar funds, investment management, cash management, budgeting, auditing, costing and calculation of indirect cost rates; and *financial accounting and reporting*: development and maintenance of the basic financial accounting and records systems and preparation of financial reports and analyses that inform the institutional community, particularly the chief executive officer and governing boards, of the financial health of the institution (Welzenbach, 1982).

Contextual Factors

The following contextual factors are addressed: (1) purposes of the chief business officer, (2) organization of business affairs, (3) nature of higher education institutions, (4) business affairs/academic affairs relationships, and (5) organizational issues.

Purposes of the Chief Business Officer. The primary responsibilities of the chief business officer are to provide leadership, manage the business and financial affairs of the institution, and keep the chief executive officer and the governing board apprised of the institution's financial condition. He or she must provide leadership; develop and recommend broad policies for all institutional functions related to business and financial matters; ensure that each unit has developed operational and strategic plans; create operating systems for business affairs functions; select, train, and manage the personnel to effectively carry out these functions; and design and implement appropriate evaluation procedures to ensure effective and efficient operation.

Organization of Business Affairs. The responsibilities and management specialties within business affairs vary depending upon the type, level, and form of support for the institution. The organizational pattern and structure within business affairs depend upon the size of the academic community, size and character of the physical plant, geographical location, external environment, history, tradition, and mission of the institution.

While the sizes and missions of colleges and universities are diverse, their administrative organizations are relatively similar. Although differences exist in sources of funds to support the activities, the accountability for stewardship and range of services offered and the relationships among the governing board, administrators, faculty, researchers, and support staff are sufficiently common to permit generalizations about evaluation in the area of business affairs.

Nature of Higher Education Institutions. Since colleges and universities are complex organizations with great diversity in scope and mission, they require administrators with a wide range of management skills. In fact, because of the intangible nature of their products, results often are not as easy to measure as they are in organizations with more tangible outcomes. In the 1980s extensive pressure exists to improve all aspects of higher education, including business affairs. The pressure for improvement is an outgrowth of several developments (Welzenbach, 1982, p. xiii):

- Movement toward efficiency in all aspects of organizational activity

- Increased interests and activity of business and industry in higher education
- Growth of the accounting profession
- A survey movement that evolved into the self-survey and modern introspective "management by objectives."

Inherent in the organizational structure and governing policies of most institutions of higher education is the collegial approach whereby the decision-making process is more diffuse and lengthy than in many other organizations. Because of the press for accountability and financial constraint, some colleges and universities have begun to follow a more businesslike model for decision making. The rational model has often been adopted and can be used to great advantage by administrators (Chaffee, 1983).

Total understanding of the academic enterprise and dedication to its mission are fundamental to the chief business officer and the manager of all business affairs or support units. Education has been a growth industry for decades, but the present and projected future conditions indicate that retrenchment and decline will be experienced by many institutions. As Easton (1976) notes, attrition in higher education will be difficult to manage because "the reverse process (of growth) is undoubtedly harder to perform," and very few of today's managers and administrators have sufficient knowledge, experience, or training to cope with business contraction (p. 5). Many of today's educational administrators were trained and educated with the growth philosophy.

Business Affairs/Academic Affairs Relationship. A unique relationship exists between business affairs units and academic units in an institution of higher education. The business affairs units exist for the purpose of providing services, products, activities, funds, and information that enhance the quality, effectiveness, and efficiency of the academic enterprise. The context for assessing the organizational behavior, performance, or outcomes of any business affairs unit should therefore include the level, type, and quality of contribution the unit makes to instructional, research, and service programs of the institution. The following considerations should be included in the review of a business affairs unit:

- Do strategic and operational plans exist within the units?
- Are these plans consistent with the strategic and operational plans for the college and university?
- Does the planning process include appropriate interactive dialogue between the provider and user of the service or product?

Because of this unique relationship, the assessment of business affairs units must go beyond the boundaries of the unit itself to determine the importance, necessity, contribution, and need for the unit.

Organizational Issues. Several organizational issues must be considered in the evaluation of business affairs units.

1. Should the service or activity be provided internally or contracted for externally? There can be no simple guideline for this issue because multiple factors must be considered and the institutional situation dictates, to a large extent, the answer. Cost, investment requirements, long-term needs, and availability of trained personnel are all sub-issues that must be assessed.

2. Will or does the activity or service provided by a unit within the institution compete directly with the private business sector? Companies in the business of providing similar services or activities for profit may not be pleased if the college or university begins to provide the same service on campus because of the negative fiscal impact it can have on their business.

3. How are decisions made concerning the allocation of resources to units in business and academic affairs? The financial needs of the academic units are normally well-known and often far exceed the resources available. The financial needs of business affairs units may not be as well-known either internally or externally. It can be difficult for business affairs units such as stores, physical plant, mail room, and risk management to compete for resources with academic units.

4. As the business affairs functions become more complicated and require highly trained personnel and sophisticated equipment, the issue of whether these operations can remain competitive with the external providers must be considered and is compounded by the lack of tax incentives for capital investment. The size of the operation may not warrant full-scale production, wages and benefits plans may not be competitive, and appropriate physical facilities may not be available.

5. Can inertia within a business affairs unit be reduced without competition and the goal of making a profit? Internal incentives may not be sufficiently strong to adequately motivate personnel in business affairs units to be effective and efficient.

Clients

Business affairs units and systems serve a wide range of clients both internal and external to the college or university. As mentioned earlier, the only purpose of these operations is to provide service and products and contribute to the primary academic mission and objectives of the institution. Thus, the evaluation of any unit or service with business affairs needs to consider user satisfaction. Each unit needs to determine the most effective approach to obtain feedback from the consumer, and both formal and informal approaches must be used on a continuous basis. User satisfaction will be discussed later.

Criteria

Accurate evaluation of business affairs units can be an arduous task, since standards and guidelines are nearly nonexistent for many of the functional areas of business affairs, in stark contrast to evaluations of academic affairs in which a plethora of standards and guidelines exist through regional and professional accreditation agencies. Criteria for both effectiveness and efficiency of business affairs units must be developed that are consistent with the outcomes of the unit being evaluated and the mission of the institution. Effectiveness criteria relate to the capability of a unit to produce the desired result, product, or outcome, while efficiency criteria relate to the ratio of useful output to total input of the unit. For example, the university printshop may be effective in that it can produce a four-color book cover. However, the university printshop would be inefficient if its cost of production is greater than the cost of purchasing the identical product from an external printshop.

Although business affairs units are diverse, the following three broad categories are suggested for establishing criteria for both effectiveness and efficiency: (1) user satisfaction, (2) financial considerations, and (3) availability of services.

User Satisfaction. Since students, faculty, and staff are the principal users of the services and products of business affairs units, they are the primary source of feedback about the degree of user satisfaction. Services may be as general as the operation of campus stores and as specific as providing accurate billing for tuition. Criteria for assessing these services and products include response time, accuracy, accessibility, ease of use, and quality. In some cases the most important criteria must be to provide the service while maintaining the desired level of confidentiality. Establishing specific criteria to assess services must rely heavily on user feedback through questionnaires, opinion surveys, informal discussions, and complaints. User satisfaction is influenced to a large extent by provider attitude and service orientation.

Financial Consideration. McCorkle and Archibald (1982) identified the general efficiency criteria of using as few resources as possible to achieve desired outcomes of acceptable quality and to achieve as large an output as possible consistent with quality for a given level of resources. The focus of these criteria is to accurately identify the resources consumed or costs incurred in relationship to the achievement of the objectives of the unit and the institution. Numerous accounting procedures and guidelines are available to evaluate the direct and indirect costs of compensation, supplies and services, travel, contractual services, and noncapital equipment.

Availability of Services. Little research has been conducted concerning the criteria for determining the wisdom of continuing or creating a unit that duplicates a service provided by an external or local vendor. The units producing services that duplicate or compete with external providers are primarily in the area of business management. Many of these services when provided by the institution are supported through user fees, determined through a cost analysis of the unit. The criteria for assessing these units may be a break-even or a price comparison for the same service provided by local businesses.

The basic question to be addressed when such services are being evaluated is, Are such services important to the attainment of the goals and mission of the institution? Providing services for the convenience of students, faculty, and staff may or may not be important enough to justify retaining or creating a unit. Also, if the university provides the service, will it be viewed as a competitor by the business community? If so, how detrimental will this be when attempting to build positive relationships with community businesses and seeking financial support from them?

Criteria for measuring effectiveness of service enterprises may be established through full cost and comparative cost analysis. Service enterprises intended to be self-supporting must establish a fee schedule to assure full cost recovery. Comparative cost analysis can be accomplished by evaluating the current rate for services offered by local businesses or other similar institutions. Institutions may find it necessary to establish break-even goals or establish profit centers for certain services in an effort to be effective.

Data Collection and Interpretation

When an evaluation of a business affairs unit should be conducted and what approach should be utilized are two questions that the chief business officer must consider. The purposes of the evaluation will affect the approach or strategy employed. There are two general approaches: regular routine monitoring of performance and ad hoc special studies of performance. Both approaches are appropriate depending on information needs, the current situation, and the specific problem or unit to be considered.

Operational Reports. The regular routine monitoring of performance includes reports that are prepared for decision makers or governing boards to reflect the current conditions of the unit and a trend analysis for the unit.

Large amounts of data are generated on a regular basis by business affairs units. Much of this information reflects activities based on internal standards of operation. Although many of these standards are subjective in nature and institution-specific, regular reports do provide useful data to the decision makers in terms of trends in level, quantity, and quality of services and the costs associated with providing the service in terms of personnel, equipment, and supplies.

It is important that a data base of quantified facts be maintained on an ongoing basis and an information system be available so that raw data can be compiled into usable information for decision makers. Unfortunately, in the past much of the data generated have not been routinely compiled and interpreted but collected and interpreted on an ad hoc basis without a common format or definition.

Sources of data must be generated and compiled on a routine basis for monthly, quarterly, and annual reports for both executive officers and governing boards from all aspects of business affairs. Specific examples of these data sources are financial statements from auxiliary enterprises, progress reports on construction activities, personnel performance reports, investment income statements, reports on physical plant operations, facility utilization reports, quarterly and annual financial statements, grant and research income reports, and formal audit reports and recommendations. The basic questions to be addressed regarding the collecting of routine data are, What is its value to the current and future operations of the institution? and Does the value justify the cost? A primary goal of any data collection and report in educational institutions must be to provide information to the decision makers that can contribute to the effectiveness and efficiency of the unit. The establishment of such a data base thus becomes a mechanism by which data are transformed into information required for operational and strategic decision making (Jones, 1982).

Ad Hoc/Special Studies

The ad hoc or special study approach can include a number of strategies for data collection and interpretation. For the purpose of this chapter, five will be reviewed: (1) external consultants, (2) internal audits, (3) blue-ribbon committees, (4) internal review committees, and (5) internal faculty expert. These strategies may be used separately or in combination, but all normally produce a set of recommendations that can be implemented.

External Consultants. External consultants are often used in the review and evaluation of business affairs of educational institutions (Gore and Wright, 1979). Many major accounting firms have specialized staff within their organizations who provide consulting services on business affairs functions in educational institutions. A consultant is normally regarded as an expert who defines, analyzes, and solves problems. The reasons for hiring consultants from outside the institution are varied, but reflect the belief that a greater degree of objectivity in judgment and evaluation can be achieved. External consultants may also prove valuable when complex issues such as benefits programs, tax reform implications, or sensitive organizational changes in structure or personnel must be studied. Often these types of problems require specialized skill and knowledge that is not needed on an ongoing basis by the institution, and, therefore, it makes sense to engage a consultant rather than increase permanent staff.

Findings and recommendations of external consultants can lead to actual cost savings, changes, and improved procedures, practices, and organizational structure. To achieve these outcomes, however, the findings and recommendations must be implemented. Considerable evidence exists that recommendations from consultants are accepted, but not implemented (Guth, 1985). The primary responsibility for implementation lies with the administration and policy makers of the institution. The services provided by the consultant will be most useful to the institution and the change implemented when a specific change is identified, a time frame is established, cost parameters are set, and extensive dialogue with internal constituents is permitted.

Internal Audits. Internal audits or operational analysis is an independent appraisal activity designed as a service for college and university administration and governing boards. It furnishes administrators and boards with analysis, appraisals, recommendations, counsel, and information concerning specific activities of an entire unit. The main objective of an internal audit is to promote effective control at reasonable costs by examining the adequacy and effectiveness of the organization's system of internal control and the quality of performance in carrying out assigned responsibilities. In an effort to render impartial and unbiased judgments, internal auditors should have free access to all records, properties, personnel, policies, plans, and procedures; however, they must remain independent of the activities they audit.

Three main types of internal audits may be performed (Sedgwick, 1986). The first, operational auditing, deals mainly with determining compliance with organizational policies and objectives and evaluating the efficiency and effectiveness of management procedures and techniques. The second, financial auditing, is perhaps the most common type of audit. This audit is designed to attest to the fairness, accuracy, and reliability of financial data. Although a financial audit deals directly with figures, the goal is to provide an accurate picture of the financial status of the institution so that precise planning can be accomplished. Finally, management auditing is designed to evaluate the activities of all levels of management for the purposes of improving organizational profitability and attaining organizational objectives through improvements in the performance of the management function. In this audit, the auditor is concerned with reviewing the content of operational policies, developed by management, management control systems, and the management decision-making process in relationship to the organizational objectives.

Blue-Ribbon Committees. Special blue-ribbon committees may be established to provide an unbiased evaluation of college or university policies and/or activities. These committees may be appointed by the administration or governing body of the institution or, as is often the case, by the executive or legislative branch of state government for public institutions or by comparable bodies for private institutions. Membership of blue-ribbon committees varies, but most include recognized and influential businesspersons, retired chief executive officers, local community leaders or representatives, staff from the institution being evaluated, and staff from other institutions of higher education.

Blue-ribbon committees are normally assigned a specific task by the body or authority that appointed them. The activities of a blue-ribbon committee vary according to the task assigned, but many function similarly to external consultants. Once the need to appoint such a committee has been established, a precise definition of the task is required; data are gathered, interpreted, and evaluated; personnel are interviewed; and recommendations are made. The implementation of specific recommendations may be the responsibility of the institutional administrators, governing boards, or authority that established the committee.

The appointment of blue-ribbon committees has become quite common during the current period of financial crisis. Both legislative and executive branches of state government have formed such committees in an effort to evaluate the missions, programs, and cost effectiveness of institutions of higher education. An advantage of using blue-ribbon committees lies in the appeal of the outside expert. Many of the members offer years of experience in the business world and are quite adept in financial management. Johnson and Marcus (1986) identify several criticisms that have been leveled at blue-ribbon committees. They can exaggerate the problems addressed, draw general rather than specific conclusions, make recommendations beyond the financial means of those who have to implement them, fail to spell out the details of their proposals, and fail to document their proposed solutions. However, despite these problems, blue-ribbon committees often offer a relatively inexpensive method for institutional review and may provide the external expertise needed when dealing with the complex issues facing business affairs.

Internal Review Committees. Committees can be established as internal review entities to evaluate the ongoing activities of business affairs units. These committees may be standing or ad hoc and can review areas such as insurance, budget, risk management, space utilization, benefits programs, and personnel administration. Membership typically includes individuals with expertise appropriate to the unit being reviewed, users of the service or product provided by the unit, staff and administrative managers from the unit, and the administrator responsible for the unit.

Committee members can provide a continuous surveillance function for business affairs administrators. Feedback on the management and performance of the business affairs unit is an important input to the business officer concerned with improving the effectiveness and efficiency of any unit within business affairs. In most cases, review committees have little or no responsibility for providing leadership to these units, but their reports allow others to be more informed.

Internal Faculty Expert. The internal expert strategy includes the use of faculty members or other staff from the institution with special expertise to evaluate business affairs units. This particular strategy has been commonly used in evaluating business affairs units in higher education. Faculties of many institutions of higher education are untapped resources that can provide leadership in the review or evaluation process. On the faculties of the professional schools of business, engineering, and education are individuals who have spent their entire careers in researching, teaching, and providing service about improved management, administration, and financial affairs within the organization. Most often these individuals, however, have used their expertise in organizations outside of the institution where they are employed.

The internal expert strategy needs careful attention and exploration, as the faculty of an institution are uniquely qualified to conduct evaluations. When institutions encourage faculty to apply their expertise in solving organizational problems, opportunities are presented for the individuals to conduct additional research and in many cases provide valuable practice or intern experiences for both graduate and undergraduate students. Most deans and chairpersons encourage faculty to apply their expertise to the real practical problems experienced by business and industry outside the institution. Why have institutions of higher education not utilized the expertise of their faculty to solve similar problems within the university? Faculty are not interested in providing service within the institution because the policies will not permit them to receive extra compensation for such service. Why should an institution hire an external consultant, who may know little about the organization and its culture, when faculty members who know the organization and its climate, culture, mission, and goals could provide the same expertise?

The following list briefly outlines the approach of capitalizing on faculty expertise within the institution to contribute to the evaluation of business affairs units:

- The area or activity to be studied is identified
- The specific problem or issue to be studied is outlined
- A review of available faculty expertise is conducted
- Selected faculty are contacted to determine interest in participation
- The faculty member refines the statement of the problem and outlines the scope and approach for the review or evaluation
- The approach for the evaluation is reviewed with the administration
- The faculty member identifies and selects graduate and undergraduate students to assist with the evaluation
- Sources of information are identified, and data are collected
- The faculty member presents preliminary findings and recom-

mendations to appropriate users and constituent groups for review and critique
- The faculty member prepares a report and presents recommendations to the administration
- The administration reviews and makes decisions concerning the implementation of recommendations
- Plans and policies are developed and procedures placed into operation.

Summary

The accurate measurement of the effectiveness and efficiency of business affairs in colleges and universities is a complex task that demands attention at all times, but especially during periods of retrenchment. Business affairs administrators are pivotal to the daily operation of an institution, and their support role for the president and governing boards has a direct impact on the future of higher education institutions.

When attempting to evaluate the effectiveness and efficiency of business affairs, it is important to deal with specific considerations that influence an education institution. Cost can be an important consideration, but cost does not stand alone. Consideration must also be given to the necessity for confidentiality of the material, user satisfaction, and the availability of the service.

Although there is great diversity among the various business affairs units, they share the common purpose of providing service to the academic enterprise. Business affairs administrators should be alert to the many factors that may influence their units. They should continually strive to improve effectiveness and efficiency through routine and ad hoc or special reviews and evaluations. The several alternative approaches and strategies for data collection and interpretation outlined in this chapter should help to determine the efficiency and effectiveness of a business affairs unit.

References

Chaffee, E. E. *Rational Decision-Making in Higher Education.* Boulder, Colo.: National Center for Higher Education Management Systems, 1983.

Easton, A. *Managing for Negative Growth: A Handbook for Practitioners.* Reston, Va.: Reston Publications, 1976.

Gore, F. J., and Wright, R. G. *The Academic Consultant Connection.* Dubuque, Iowa: Kendall/Hunt, 1979.

Guth, W. D. (ed.). *Handbook of Business Strategy.* Boston: Warren, Gorman & Lamont, 1985.

Johnson, J. R., and Marcus, L. R. *Blue-Ribbon Commissions and Higher Education.* ASHE-ERIC Higher Education Report, no. 2. Washington, D.C.: Association for the Study of Citizen Education, 1986.

Jones, D. P. *Data and Information for Executive Decisions in Higher Education.* Boulder, Colo.: National Center for Higher Education Management Systems, 1982.

McCorkle, C. O., Jr., and Archibald, S. O. *Management and Leadership in Higher Education: Applying Modern Techniques of Planning, Resource Management, and Evaluation.* San Francisco: Jossey-Bass, 1982.

Sedgwick, K. (ed.). *Proceedings of the Twenty-Ninth Annual Conference.* Ogden, Utah: Association of College and University Auditors, 1986.

Welzenbach, L. F. (ed.). *College & University Business Administration.* Washington, D.C.: National Association of College and University Business Officers, 1982.

Alan T. Seagren is vice-president for administration at the University of Nebraska, a comprehensive system consisting of three campuses. He remains active as a professor of educational administration, teaching courses in planning and higher education finance and advising graduate students.

Gary A. Miller is dean of academic affairs at the Los Angeles College of Chiropractic. He has had extensive experience in planning and evaluating academic and business programs in institutions of higher education.

Although intercollegiate athletics are harder to evaluate than other campus services and programs, administrators have an obligation to examine the functioning of their athletic programs and the relationship of sports to their institutions' educational missions.

Beyond Ws and Ls: Evaluating Intercollegiate Athletics Programs

Barbara Gross Davis

In recent years, intercollegiate athletics have generated some of the most scandalous and difficult problems facing colleges and universities. Illegal recruiting, compromised admissions standards, athletes kept eligible with nonacademic courses, gambling and point-shaving, drug abuse—newspapers are filled with horror stories of troubled athletics programs.

Such headlines reflect the general inattentiveness of academic administrators and faculty to their own sports programs. Because regular institutional evaluations tend to exclude athletic departments (Hanford, 1979), few universities and colleges critically examine the functioning of their athletics programs and the relationship of sports to their institutions' educational missions. Unless a scandal breaks, many campus officials are satisfied by incidental or anecdotal information and a look at their teams' win-loss records.

This chapter offers advice on evaluating the functioning and effectiveness of intercollegiate athletics programs. Although many of the examples concern Division I-A football and men's basketball—the most visible and perhaps the most troubled of programs—the suggestions can be applied to nonrevenue sports in men's and women's athletics.

J. F. Wergin and L. A. Braskamp (eds.). *Evaluating Administrative Services and Programs.*
New Directions for Institutional Research, no. 56. San Francisco: Jossey-Bass, Winter 1987.

Initial Considerations

For several reasons, intercollegiate athletics are harder to evaluate than other campus services and programs. First, few areas of campus life arouse such intense feelings. Athletics have a large and active constituency: Many college presidents report that mail about athletics exceeds correspondence on any other topic (Bok, 1985). As a result, discussions about, let alone attempts to evaluate, athletics are constrained by political considerations. Gilley and Hickey (1986) describe the plight of a university president who recommended to the trustees that the athletic director be fired. The trustees balked—and instead requested and received the resignation of the president.

Second, access to valuable comparative information is difficult. Few campuses systematically collect or candidly report data on their sports programs. Administrators are closemouthed about the graduation rates of athletes, grade-point averages, athletic budgets, and the like. This general silence prevents institutions from making comparisons with their peers.

Third, athletics is big-time business and the stakes are high. Television revenues and national attention are bestowed on winning programs, and some administrators believe that donations from alumni are positively associated with athletic success. Why risk an evaluation that may uncover blemishes?

Fourth, institutions may be reluctant to undertake evaluations on their own without a consensus about policies and practices at the conference, regional, or national level. Adopting rigorous self-evaluation procedures, they argue, may place universities at a competitive disadvantage unless their peer institutions are willing to do the same.

While these are formidable obstacles, they should not deter administrators from developing suitable evaluation mechanisms. Even if the athletic program functions as an independent entity, it is best evaluated in a manner consistent with the practices for evaluating other campus programs.

Although there is no agreement on the best methods to conduct or use evaluation in higher education (Shapiro, 1986), there are basic principles: substantial faculty involvement, emphasis on academic concerns, clearly stated purposes for the evaluation, and systematic procedures that are explained to all involved. And, like any other evaluation, the assessment of athletics programs will require decisions about the types of information to be gathered, the methods of gathering the information, the standards and criteria for making worthy judgments, and the means by which the information will be analyzed, interpreted, disseminated, and used.

Paradigms for Evaluating Athletics Programs

A useful paradigm for orienting an evaluation is the Key Evaluation Checklist (Scriven, 1981), which can be applied to any type of program or support service (Davis, Scriven, and Thomas, in press; Davis and Humphreys, 1985). Among the dimensions of a program to be considered in a comprehensive evaluation are:
- The context in which the program operates
- The resources available to the program
- The legal, ethical, and political considerations affecting the program
- The needs of participants, nonparticipants, staff, and other constituencies
- The organization and administration of the program
- The intended and unintended effects of the program
- The fiscal and nonfiscal costs (such as opportunity costs)
- A comparison of the program to similar efforts at comparable institutions.

From these general categories, administrators can begin to formulate the specific questions that the evaluation is to address.

Questions can also be generated from checklists provided by the National Collegiate Athletic Association (NCAA) (1981, 1985). The NCAA's self-study guides itemize questions in nine areas (a sample question is listed here for each area):

1. *Institutional purpose and athletics philosophy.* Is there a written statement of philosophy for athletics programs?

2. *Authority of the chief executive officer (CEO) in personnel and financial affairs.* Does the director of athletics report directly to the CEO or to a senior administrator or committee who reports directly to the CEO?

3. *Organization and administration of the athletics program.* Is the faculty periodically consulted on institutional policies and practices that affect the operation of intercollegiate athletics?

4. *Athletics program finances.* Do institutional policies require all revenues of the athletics program to be processed by an independent office?

5. *Employment of athletics program personnel.* Are all coaches required to participate in continuing education programs regarding NCAA and conference rules?

6. *Sports program.* Has a recent study determined whether the time student-athletes devote to athletics intrudes on satisfactory progress toward their degrees?

7. *Recruiting, admissions, and eligibility.* Are all applications by prospective student-athletes handled by admissions personnel not affiliated with the athletics program?

8. *Services for student-athletes.* Has the program of academic tutoring and counseling for student-athletes been reviewed within the past year by campus officials not affiliated with the athletics program?

9. *Student-athlete profiles.* If the institution admits student-athletes who do not meet regular admissions requirements, does it routinely collect and assess class enrollments, class attendance, midterm grades, final grades, and progress toward a degree?

Of course, an institution's specific purpose in evaluating its athletics program will shape the questions that are asked, the data that are gathered, and the use that is made of the evaluation information. For example, administrators may need information about a particular topic in order to gauge campus awareness and support of the athletics program, to identify why attendance at some athletic events is low, or to determine whether athletics program personnel are operating compatibly with the academic goals of the institution.

The following recommendations for evaluating intercollegiate athletics are arranged in four broad categories: the philosophy and culture of athletics at the institution; institutional control, organization, and administration of the athletics program; health, welfare, and academic support of student-athletes; and compliance with NCAA and conference rules and regulations.

Philosophy and Culture of the Institution

A key task in evaluating an athletic program is to determine the place of athletics in the school's value system: What does the institution expect of its athletics program? Does the program function with integrity? Is a proper balance between athletics and academics communicated to students, faculty, staff, alumni, and the public?

Data can be gathered by examining the campus administration's public statements about the athletics program, materials distributed to students, and newspaper coverage; by surveying the campus community about the role of athletics; and by analyzing the level of effort and resources that the institution devotes to athletic enterprises.

On the question of expectations, most campus administrators agree on the general goals of fielding competitive teams that maintain academic and moral integrity. *Competitive* is usually taken to mean that a team has its share of winning games and exciting, well-coached losses. But program integrity is harder to define. Clearly, integrity requires that the program be in compliance with NCAA rules and regulations. But what are the criteria for academic integrity in admissions, for example? How many student-athletes who do not meet the school's regular admissions requirements may be admitted without compromising academic integrity? And how far below those regular admissions standards may student-athletes fall?

Discussions of integrity also include questions of balance. Each school must decide the relative emphasis that intercollegiate athletics will have in the overall life of the campus. At one end of the spectrum are the Ivy League schools, which ban off-season practice, offer no athletic scholarships, and do not relax their admission standards for athletes (Lederman, 1986). Several other institutions have recently adopted this model, for example, members of the new Colonial League.

At the other end of the spectrum are schools whose identity and culture seem dominated by their athletics programs. Two recent examples will suffice. In explaining why his Division I-AA school hired a big-name football coach and moved up to Division I-A, a university president contended that the new status and attendant publicity would help his school in recruiting student and faculty, encouraging increased alumni contributions, and promoting campus spirit. (Others, of course, argue that such ends are best achieved by directly allocating funds to attract top-flight faculty and students.) At another institution, winning was not enough: The football coach, whose teams made bowl appearances in three of the last four years, was dismissed because his teams were unsuccessful against the university's archrivals.

What can a university or college do to achieve a proper balance between athletics and academics? Those who have addressed this issue agree that collective action by university presidents or federal intervention may be required to effect major reforms ("Punt the Pretense," 1986; Gilley and Hickey, 1986; Bok, 1985; Mihalich, 1984). Among their recommendations are (1) stabilize athletic budgets; (2) curtail the activities and influence of athletic associations or booster clubs; (3) shorten athletic seasons, including practices, to a single semester for each sport; (4) exempt students from courses in the semester in which they play, and exempt them from practice in the semester in which they study; (5) give athletes four years of athletic eligibility and six years of financial assistance; (6) place limits on the quota of scholarships available to institutions unless the graduation rate for athletes matches that of the student body overall; (7) deny tax deductions for gifts to athletic departments that graduate less than 75 percent of the student-athletes on scholarships; (8) eliminate separate dormitories for student-athletes; (9) eliminate noncourses; (10) involve presidents and chancellors more actively in athletics programs; and (11) include athletics programs in the standard accreditation procedures of colleges and universities.

Institutional Control: Organization, Administration, Finance

An important evaluation task is to examine the level and type of institutional control of the athletics program. Is the president or chancellor well-informed about athletics program, particularly about the academic records of entering athletes and the academic progress of continuing athletes? What is the relationship between academic faculty and athletics personnel? How well do they understand one another's missions? What opportunities are provided for collaborative activities?

One decisive measure of the relationship between athletics and an institution's educational mission is the way in which athletics are financed. Hanford (1979) classifies the control and administration of athletics programs as internal, adjunct, or auxiliary, according to financing. Internal athletics programs are supported from general funds and are subject to the same rules for resource allocation as other campus units and departments. Adjunct programs are viewed as extracurricular activities—neither integral to the educational process nor separate from it—deserving of some institutional support, similar to student performance groups or the campus newspaper. Auxiliary programs, in contrast, are treated as separate, financially self-sufficient enterprises.

As Hanford points out, the auxiliary model leads to an uneasy relationship between the institution's constituencies and the administration of the athletics program. Since auxiliary programs do not report directly to academic administrators, they are not under effective academic supervision and do not necessarily share in the educational culture, academic mission, or institutional goals set by the chancellor or president. Further, as Gilley and Hickey (1986) note, athletics programs with auxiliary status are more likely to be mismanaged and susceptible to rules violations.

What does it mean to be under academic control? First, that admissions decisions are made by the regular admissions office and not by the athletic department. Second, that academic issues such as tutoring and advising are given high priority and attention. Third, that athletic policies are set by the campus's chief executive officer and that well-defined lines of authority exist.

At some schools, administrative and faculty oversight is enforced by a faculty board or committee that sets and monitors policy in intercollegiate athletics (Becker, Sparks, Choi, and Sell, 1986). Through such mechanisms, faculty define policies that benefit the education and welfare of students while consulting generally on practices that affect the operation of athletics. Some conferences mandate faculty boards for all member institutions.

In addition to institutional control, the evaluation should examine the internal administration of the athletics program: logistics, practices, scheduling, travel activities, and so on. Procedures that the athletics program has established to monitor its operations and effectiveness should also be reviewed.

Finally, personnel practices should be assessed. The principles used to evaluate the job performance of athletic personnel might parallel those used to evaluate faculty: clearly stated purposes for the evaluation, a variety of data from many different sources, and so on. Further, athletic personnel, as members of the campus community, should be bound by the same rules of conduct as the faculty. For example, universities typically have established conflict-of-interest policies governing ways in which a faculty member can be compensated for outside activities. Similar guidelines could be developed for coaches and, indeed, the NCAA recently adopted a rule requiring coaches to disclose outside income from summer camps, lecturing, and product endorsements.

Porto (1984) describes a broad set of criteria for evaluating coaches, pointing out that coaches who believe their jobs depend solely on winning may adopt a "win at all costs" philosophy that paves the way for abuses and violations. The NCAA (1985) urges institutions to develop a set of written criteria for evaluating the job performance of athletic personnel. They suggest, for example, that coaches be evaluated on their observance of NCAA rules, academic performance of student-athletes, and the health and safety of athletes. To this list one might add a coach's understanding of the institution's academic mission and the ways in which athletics contributes to that mission.

Beyond these criteria, Porto (1984) suggests examining coaches' perceptions of job security. Insecure coaches, he notes, are more likely to skirt recruiting regulations, publicly criticize players, place excessive demands on players' time, order injured players to play, and arbitrarily purge assistant coaches.

Data for addressing these issues can come from interviewing or surveying program staff, student-athletes, and faculty board members; reviewing program budgets and operations; and examining program materials and documents.

Services and Resources for Student-Athletes

The goals of most institutions with respect to student-athletes are similar: to keep them eligible; to ensure that they receive a proper education, do well academically, and graduate in impressive numbers; and to help them develop socially, academically, and athletically. The plight of the student-athlete in meeting these goals is well-documented (Rhatigan, 1984; Purdy, Eitzen, and Hufnagel, 1982; Whitner and Myers, 1986). Consider a typical basketball player. Away games force him to miss 15-20 percent of his classes, yet he is expected to meet the independent demands of athletic and academic responsibilities while coping with the pressures of public performance (Rhatigan, 1984).

Institutions that recruit athletes have an obligation to provide the resources and support services these students need to succeed, and students who are recruited to represent the university have a right to expect that they will succeed in both the classroom and on the playing field. As Bok

(1985, p. 128) puts it, "What could be more offensive to the ideals of an educational institution than to admit substantial numbers of unqualified students each year, pay them to subject themselves to a forty-hour athletic schedule and then abandon them without a degree or serious preparation for a career after their eligibility expires?"

A comprehensive academic support program for student-athletes would include:

- Orientation sessions to acquaint students with the services and procedures of the university
- Diagnostic services to identify academic problem areas early on
- Well-coordinated advising, preferably by advisers affiliated with the academic program
- Tutoring or academic assistance, as needed, including summer preparatory programs
- Counseling for academic or personal concerns
- Liaison procedures for dealing with campus services such as housing, financial aid, registration, and the like.

While few administrators would quibble with this list, many might veto the costs of mounting such support programs or question the wisdom of allocating disproportionate campus resources to a small subgroup. But if a school is unable or unwilling to provide student-athletes with the resources they need to become successful members of the academic community, then the institution must reexamine its admissions practices and athletic goals.

Further, the responsibilities for academic support services must be explicitly communicated to students, coaches, and faculty. Problems will occur if the athletics program views the institution as responsible for ensuring that student-athletes remain eligible and receive an education while the faculty consider these matters the students' responsibility, and if students believe it is up to the athletics program to take care of them. Researchers (Hurley and Cunningham, 1984) agree that the message to students must be: We want you to succeed academically and to graduate; we will do all that we can to help you, but ultimately whether you graduate is up to you.

The following questions are crucial to the evaluation of academic support services:

- Are academic assistance programs staffed by qualified professionals and adequately budgeted?
- Do academic assistance programs offer a suitable range of services?
- What support is provided for underprepared students to bring them up to campus academic standards?
- What arrangements for study time are provided and how are they coordinated with students' classes?

- What arrangements are made to monitor student-athletes' academic performance and to detect early warning signs of poor work?
- In what ways do the coaches emphasize the importance of academic achievement and support services to student-athletes?

In addition to looking at services, it is important to evaluate the academic outcomes of the athletics program. What is the educational attainment (college grade-point average and graduation rate) of students who participate in athletics (by gender, ethnicity, scholarship-nonscholarship, and by sport)? How do these figures compare to the rates of nonathletes? Research on this topic is mixed (Purdy, Eitzen, and Hufnagel, 1982), with some studies finding comparable levels of attainment and others indicating that athletes have lower grades and graduation rates than other nonathlete counterparts. The evaluation should also determine who checks the academic progress of student-athletes, to whom the information is reported, and at what point coaches are informed about a student's academic difficulties.

Finally, the evaluation should examine the health and welfare of students. Are training procedures adequate, especially physical exams, injury prevention, treatment, and rehabilitation? Are the equipment and facilities adequate to prevent injury, ensure health and safety, and promote performance?

Data to answer questions raised in this section can be provided by interviews or surveys of student-athletes, program staff, and faculty; examination of transcripts and student records; observation of facilities, equipment, and procedures; and review of program materials. The NCAA (1985) also suggests exit interviews for all student-athletes who drop out or leave without graduating.

Compliance with NCAA Conference Rules and Regulations

The NCAA's policies and regulations are intended to promote proper behavior among institutions on and off the field. An evaluation of an athletics program should examine a program's procedures for complying with NCAA and conference rules and should assess the activities of the faculty athletics representative to the NCAA. What is the role of the NCAA faculty athletic representative within the institution? Who establishes the role? To whom does the representative report, and what are his or her essential activities? How does the representative view his or her position (for example, informal versus formal)? Is this representative provided with the necessary resources to carry out his or her responsibilities? Are there adequate procedures to ensure that the athletics program is kept current on new regulations?

Interviews with athletic personnel, the NCAA faculty representative, and other faculty involved in providing academic support services and advising to athletes can provide data to answer these questions.

Conclusion

Academic and athletics are not inimical. The goal of most universities is to excel at both: to maintain institutional integrity and a competitive program that addresses the academic and developmental needs of student-athletes. Given the importance and visibility of athletics programs, campus administrators have an obligation to both individual athletes and the campus community to sponsor ongoing evaluations of the performance of athletics programs on and off the field.

References

Becker, S. L., Sparks, W. G., Choi, H. C., and Sell, L. "Intercollegiate Athletic Committees: Dimensions of Influence." *Journal of Higher Education*, 1986, 57 (4), 431–441.

Bok, D. "Intercollegiate Athletics." In J. B. Bennett and J. W. Peltason (eds.), *Contemporary Issues in Higher Education*. Washington, D.C.: American Council on Education, 1985.

Davis, B. G., and Humphreys, S. *Evaluating Intervention Programs*. New York: Teachers College Press, 1985.

Davis, B. G., Scriven, M., and Thomas, S. *The Evaluation of Composition Instruction*. New York: Teachers College Press, in press.

Gilley, J. W., and Hickey, A. *Administration of University Athletic Programs*. Fairfax, Va.: George Mason University, 1986.

Hanford, G. H. "Controversies in College Sports." *Educational Record*, 1979, 60 (4), 351–366.

Hurley, R. B., and Cunningham, R. L. "Providing Academic and Psychological Services for College Athletes." In A. Shriberg and F. R. Brodzinski (eds.), *Rethinking Services for College Athletes*. New Directions for Student Services, no. 28. San Francisco: Jossey-Bass, 1984.

Lederman, D. "The Ivy League at 30." *Chronicle of Higher Education*, November 19, 1986, p. 1.

Mihalich, J. C. "College Sports: Decisions for Survival." In A. Shriberg and F. R. Brodzinski (eds.), *Rethinking Services for College Athletes*. New Directions for Student Services, no. 28. San Francisco: Jossey-Bass, 1984.

National Collegiate Athletic Association. *Evaluation of Intercollegiate Athletics: A Suggested Guide for the Process of Self-Study*. Mission, Kans.: National Collegiate Athletic Association, 1981.

National Collegiate Athletic Association. *Guide to Institutional Self-Study to Enhance Integrity in Intercollegiate Athletics*. Mission, Kans.: National Collegiate Athletic Association, 1985.

Porto, B. L. "When Coaches Are Teachers, Athletes Will Be Students." *Liberal Education*, 1984, 70 (3), 231–233.

"Punt the Pretense." *New Republic*, September 8, 1986, pp. 7–8.

Purdy, D. A., Eitzen, D. S., and Hufnagel, R. "Are Athletes Also Students?" *Social Problems*, 1982, 29, 439–448.

Rhatigan, J. J. "Serving Two Masters: The Plight of the College Student-Athlete." In A. Shriberg and F. R. Brodzinski (eds.), *Rethinking Services for College Athletes.* New Directions for Student Services, no. 28. San Francisco: Jossey-Bass, 1984.

Scriven, M. *Evaluation Thesaurus.* Pt. Reyes, Calif.: Edgepress, 1981.

Shapiro, J. Z. "Evaluation Research and Educational Decision-Making." In J. C. Smart (ed.), *Higher Education: Handbook of Theory and Research.* Vol. 2. New York: Agathon Press, 1986.

Whitner, P. A., and Myers, R. C. "Academics and an Athlete." *Journal of Higher Education,* 1986, 57 (6), 659-672.

Barbara Gross Davis is director of the Office of Educational Development, University of California, Berkeley.

The evaluation of student support services employs objectives, strategies, and traditional and nontraditional measures.

Evaluating Student Support Services

William E. Sedlacek

Despite the general call for the virtues of evaluation stated throughout this sourcebook, there are some unique reasons to evaluate student support services. Student support services comprise tutoring, counseling, academic skill development, and a variety of services we call special programs for students who are deemed in need of something beyond what is provided by student services in general. The variety and nature of these programs lead to the first important purpose for evaluation in this area: needs assessment.

Often students are assigned or encouraged to seek such services because their traditional indicators of academic success (for example, standardized test scores, previous grades, courses taken) indicate that they do not appear competitive with other students at their institution. But often little if any diagnostic information is provided on what particular combination of services would be best for a given student. Because the student is by definition nontraditional, it is crucial that the needs of each student be evaluated and that the services offered be matched to those needs.

A second reason to evaluate support services is that we need to know what works and what does not. What helps the student, and what is a waste of time? Nontraditional students are short on resources and time; we cannot afford to waste either. Evaluation will also help with allocation of program resources. At a time when funding is scarce and many services are under scrutiny and competing for hard money with other programs, it is important to relate costs to services. For instance, if a program goal is retention, or graduation of students, linking needs and costs to these outcomes is an effective means of helping a program compete for funds.

Also, data can help promote a program and make it more visible to the institution or to relevant others. Data speak; cries of need often do not. Program staff need to maintain control of the evaluation or someone else will. Initiating and maintaining an effective evaluation program increases the probability that someone who understands the program will be evaluating it. Evaluation will take place regardless of intention or lack of planning.

Aside from the goal of student development, there is the goal of employee development. Working in support programs can be frustrating, and it is easy to feel that no one cares whether you succeed. Evaluation can provide needed direction and support for employees. Feeling part of a program, rather than an ad hoc collection of events, is necessary in providing good student support services.

General Principles of Evaluation

The principles of evaluation that would apply to any good evaluation are equally applicable here. The reader is referred to other chapters in this book, or other references for a detailed discussion (for example, Isaac and Michael, 1981; Rossi, Freeman, and Wright, 1979; Kuh, 1979; or Stufflebeam and others, 1971). An oversimplification of the three steps in program evaluation is offered by Isaac and Michael (1981). They suggest that, first, objectives be stated in measurable or observable terms. Next, the strategies or activities that will be implemented to attain each objective should be stated. Finally the measures by which attainment of each objective will be determined should be selected and employed.

The purpose of this chapter will be to discuss issues that may be relevant when evaluating student support service programs.

Evaluating Traditional Variables

Student support service programs have often been concerned with providing skill development in several academic areas, which will be briefly presented and discussed.

Study Skills. In her review of the literature on evaluations of study skills courses, Entwisle (1960) concluded that a study skills course will usually be followed by an improvement in grades, although courses were most beneficial for students who took them voluntarily. When motivation was experimentally controlled, those students who took the study skills course improved their grades more than those who did not. The gains in grades were not necessarily related to course content or duration.

The more recent literature suggests that programs that have multiple objectives and are evaluated as such are most effective. For instance, programs that include study skills along with planning and self-monitoring skills have been shown to be effective (for example, Greiner and Karoly, 1976; Kirschenbaum and Perri, 1982; Richards and Perri, 1978). Including components such as reading effectiveness (Robinson, 1970) and classroom skills such as techniques on how to take notes (Pauk, 1962) have also been shown to affect grades when combined with study skills.

Using evaluations from participants and leaders, Malett, Kirschenbaum, and Humphrey (1983) found that an eleven-session, peer-facilitated, study improvement program yielded several conclusions that one might consider in other evaluations. Technique-oriented sessions, particularly those involving detailed handouts and practice sessions, were judged most effective. Also, work on values clarification was found to be useful. Questionnaires designed to reflect goals for each session were constructed by the investigators.

Reading. Research on the effectiveness of reading instruction appears to have shifted from a central emphasis on cognitive skills to approaches that emphasize cognitive strategies, self-management, and motivation (Paris, Wixson, and Palinscar, 1986). Day (1980) used four treatment conditions: self-management, in which students were given guidelines; rules, in which students were given specific rules to follow; rules plus self-management; and a fourth condition that included rules, self-management, and information on how to evaluate effectiveness in implementing rules. The rules plus self-management condition was best for most college students, with the most explicit condition most helpful for students with learning problems. Performance on written summaries of material was used as the criterion.

Johnston and Winograd (1985) have used the term *passive failure* to explain unmotivated readers. Passive failure seems to be the perception that responses and outcomes are independent; students do not blame themselves for failure or take credit for success. Passive failure is promoted by assigning a reading that is too difficult for poor readers, using criticism rather than praise, and treating successful students more favorably than others (Paris, Wixson, and Palinscar, 1986). Johnston and Winograd (1985) suggest that providing easier tasks, evaluating less frequently, promoting awareness of response-outcome relations, teaching students to attribute success or failure to particular reading strategies, and focusing student attention on the processes of reading rather than normative outcomes are ways to reduce passive failure.

While some of the references cited here have focused on students whose reading level is below the college level, the principles generated appear worth considering in conducting evaluations for college students with reading problems.

Writing. The model of Bereiter and Scardamalia (1986), which contains six levels of inquiry in research in the composing process, questions that might be asked, and typical methods employed in answering the questions, should prove useful in evaluating writing programs. Bereiter and Scardamalia particularly caution against becoming too focused on empirical variable testing. The interest in finding correlates of good and poor writing, and programs that try to teach the difference, can lead to an atheoretical and nondevelopmental approach to evaluation research. Their model can be used to categorize the type of evaluation being conducted and should help one move to higher levels of inquiry.

Evaluating Nontraditional Variables

A model that has been shown to be related to the success of nontraditional students in higher education is presented here as the basis for the evaluation of student support services. Sedlacek and Brooks (1976) identified seven variables from the literature that seemed to predict the success of students who had had other than the traditional white middle- or upper-middle-class experience prior to college matriculation. Tracey and Sedlacek (1984, 1985, 1987) demonstrated the reliability and validity of a measure of the seven variables plus an eighth one. The noncognitive questionnaire (NCQ) has been shown to predict the grades, retention, and gradution of black students up to six years after initial matriculation. Boyer and Sedlacek (1987a) found the NCQ to be predictive for international students, and White and Sedlacek (1986) found validity for the NCQ in predicting the success of specially admitted students who did not meet regular admissions standards. Additionally, Boyer and Sedlacek (1987b) and Arbona and Sedlacek (1987) have shown that the NCQ predicts whether international students and U.S. students, white or black, will use the support services provided.

The NCQ could be used to assess change and development on the eight dimensions using a pre- and post-test model, ideally with a control group. It would also be possible to make behavioral observations of students, with or without formal questionnaires or checklists. A discussion of the characteristics of high- and low-scoring students on each of the eight variables follows.

Positive Self-Concept or Confidence. High scorers feel confident of making it through graduation and make positive statements about themselves. They expect to do well in academic and nonacademic areas and assume they can handle new situations or challenges.

Low scorers express reasons why they might have to leave school and are not sure they have the ability to make it. They feel other students are more capable, and expect to get marginal grades. They feel they will have trouble balancing personal and academic life. They avoid new challenges or situations.

Realistic Self-Appraisal. High scorers appreciate and accept rewards as well as consequences of poor performance. They understand that reinforcement is imperfect and do not overreact to positive or negative feedback. They have developed a system of using feedback to alter behavior.

Low scorers are not sure how evaluations are done in school and overreact to the most recent reinforcement (positive and negative), rather than seeing it in a larger context. They do not know how they are doing in classes until grades are out. They do not have a good idea of how peers would rate their performance.

Understands and Deals With Racism. High scorers understand the role of the "system" in their life and how it treats minority persons, often unintentionally. They have developed a method of assessing the cultural and racial demands of the system and responding accordingly: assertively, if the gain is worth it, passively, if the gain is small or the situation ambiguous. They do not blame others for their problems or appear as a "Pollyanna" who does not see racism.

Low scorers are not sure how the "system" works and are preoccupied with racism or do not feel racism exists. They blame others for their problems and react with the same intensity to large and small issues concerned with race. They do not have a successful method of handling racism that does not interfere with their personal and academic development.

Prefers Long-Range Goals to Short-Term or Immediate Needs. High scorers can set goals and proceed for some time without reinforcement. They show patience and can see partial fulfillment of a longer-term goal. They are future- and past-oriented and do not see just immediate issues or problems. They show evidence of planning in academic and non-academic areas.

Low scorers show little ability to set and accomplish goals and are likely to proceed without clear direction. They rely on others to determine outcomes and live in the present. They do not have a plan for approaching a course, school in general, an activity, and so on. The goals they have tend to be vague and unrealistic.

Availability of Strong Support Person. High scorers have identified and received help, support, and encouragement from one or more specific individuals. They do not rely solely on their own resources to solve problems. They are not loners and are willing to admit they need help when it is appropriate.

Low scorers show no evidence of turning to others for help. They usually have no single support person, mentor, or close adviser. They do not talk about their problems and feel they can handle things on their own. Access to a previous support person may be reduced or eliminated, and they are not aware of the importance of a support person.

Successful Leadership Experience. High scorers have shown evidence of influencing others in academic or nonacademic areas. They are comfortable providing advice and direction to others and have served as mediators in disputes or disagreements among colleagues. They are comfortable taking action where it is called for.

Low scorers show no evidence that others turn to them for advice or direction. They are nonassertive and do not take the initiative. They are overly cautious and avoid controversy. They are not well-known by their peers.

Demonstrated Community Service. High scorers are identified with a group that is cultural, racial, or geographic. They have specific and long-term relationships in a community and have been active in community activities over a period of time. They have accomplished specific goals in a community setting.

Low scorers tend to have no involvement in a cultural, racial, or geographical group or community. They have limited activities of any kind and are fringe members of any group to which they belong. They engage more in solitary rather than group activities (academic or nonacademic).

Knowledge Acquired in a Field. High scorers know about a field or area that they have not formally studied in school. They have a nontraditional, possibly culturally or racially based view of a field or profession. They have developed innovative ways to acquire information about a given subject or field.

Low scorers appear to know little about fields or areas that they have not studied in school. They show no evidence of learning from community or nonacademic activities and are traditional in their approach to learning. They have not received credit-by-examination for courses and may not be aware of credit-by-examination possibilities.

Implementing the Evaluation

Following is an example of how one might implement an evaluation of a student support service in the context of the above discussion. Step one requires stating the program objectives in clear, concise, observable terms. Is the goal to raise grades? If so, in specific courses or overall? For a semester or long-term? An example of a clearly stated goal is: The objective of the program is to raise the grades of all participants in program X to a minimum of a C in English 101 in the spring semester. Another common objective of student support programs is retention, which must be specifically defined. For instance, do we mean retention for a semester until graduation, in one major, in good academic standing, excluding those who transfer, or for those who drop out and reenter? One may achieve quite different results depending on how the objective is defined.

Another important category of program objectives, particularly when combined with academic outcome variables, concerns student attitudes and feelings of self-worth. Do students in the program feel part of the larger student body? Are they motivated to continue their education? Do they feel they can make it in school? These and many other related questions could be turned into program objectives.

For instance, an objective might be to increase students' knowledge about how to handle racism, since this variable is related to grades for minority students.

Step two involves matching intervention strategies to objectives. Too often program content is determined by tradition or expectations that are not based on the best information available. For instance, research findings suggest that programs involving multiple content areas are probably more effective than those focusing on a single and more limited content area. For example, we might choose a multiple-session strategy that involves peer facilitators and focuses on study techniques with active practice sessions and handouts as suggested by Malett, Kirschenbaum, and Humphrey (1983). Or for an objective concerning racism, discussions, exercises, group problem solving on racism, and how to define and deal with racism might be added to the series of sessions (for example, Sedlacek and Brooks, 1976). A key point is that no program content should be implemented if it is not directly tied to a program objective.

Step three in the evaluation process is to select the measures that one would use to determine whether the objectives of the program have been met. If the objective deals with grades, a simple and direct measure is available. If the objective is more intermediate (for example, study habits or understanding racism), other measures must be adopted or developed. It is preferable to use a measure already available; for example, Malett, Kirschenbaum, and Humphrey (1983) present questionnaires to assess study skills; Tracey and Sedlacek (1987) developed a measure assessing ability to handle racism. Developing home-grown measures may be complicated and time-consuming, although excellent technical resources are available (Isaac and Michael, 1981; Sudman and Bradburn, 1982).

Conclusion

The purpose of this chapter was to present some ideas and approaches for evaluating support services. Organizing the evaluation in terms of objectives, strategies, and measures is a useful beginning step. Further categorization by traditional and nontraditional variables should help further specify the nature of the evaluation. Finally, attention to specific problems or models within this framework such as consideration of passive failures in teaching reading, or use of long-range goals as a noncognitive variable, should enhance the thoroughness of an evaluation project. There are many additional variables one might study in student support programs, including math skills and specific content areas such as history, art, or biology. It is hoped that some of the information provided here will provide a beginning for evaluating student support services in these or other areas.

References

Arbona, C., and Sedlacek, W. E. *Correlates of Helpseeking Behavior of Minority Students.* Counseling Center Research Report no. 3-87. College Park: University of Maryland, 1987.

Bereiter, C., and Scardamalia, M. "Levels of Inquiry into the Nature of Expertise in Writing." In E. Z. Rothkopf (ed.), *Review of Research in Education.* Vol. 13. Washington, D.C.: American Educational Research Association, 1986.

Boyer, S. P., and Sedlacek, W. E. *Predicting Academic Success of International Students Using Noncognitive Variables.* Counseling Center Research Report no. 1-87. College Park: University of Maryland, 1987a.

Boyer, S. P., and Sedlacek, W. E. *Predicting Counseling Behavior of International Students Using Noncognitive Variables.* Counseling Center Research Report no. 2-87. College Park: University of Maryland, 1987b.

Day, J. D. "Training Summarization Skills: A Comparison of Teaching Methods." Unpublished doctoral dissertation, University of Illinois, Urbana, 1980.

Entwisle, D. R. "Evaluations of Study Skills Courses: A Review." *Journal of Educational Research,* 1960, *53,* 247-251.

Greiner, J. M., and Karoly, P. "Effects of Self-Control Training on Study Activity and Academic Performance: An Analysis of Self-Monitoring, Self-Reward, and Systematic Planning Components." *Journal of Counseling Psychology,* 1976, *23,* 495-502.

Isaac, S., and Michael, W. B. *Handbook in Research and Evaluation.* (2nd ed.) San Diego: Edits, 1981.

Johnston, P. H., and Winograd, P. N. "Passive Failure in Reading." *Journal of Reading Behavior,* 1985, *17,* 279-301.

Kirschenbaum, D. S., and Perri, M. G. "Improving Academic Competence in Adults: A Review of Recent Research." *Journal of Counseling Psychology,* 1982, *29,* 79-94.

Kuh, G. D. (ed.). *Evaluation in Student Affairs.* Washington, D.C.: American College Personnel Association, 1979.

Malett, S. D., Kirschenbaum, D. S., and Humphrey, L. L. "Description and Subjective Evaluation of an Objectively Successful Study Improvement Program." *Personnel and Guidance Journal,* 1983, *62,* 341-345.

Paris, S. G., Wixson, K. K., and Palinscar, A. S. "Instruction Approaches to Reading Comprehension." In E. Z. Rothkopf (ed.), *Review of Research in Education.* Vol. 13. Washington, D.C.: American Educational Research Association, 1986.

Pauk, W. *How to Study in College.* Boston: Houghton Mifflin, 1962.

Richards, C. S., and Perri, M. G. "Do Self-Control Treatments Last? An Evaluation of Behavioral Problem Solving and Faded Counselor Contact as Treatment Maintenance Strategies." *Journal of Counseling Psychology*, 1978, *25*, 376-383.

Robinson, F. *Effective Study*. (4th ed.) New York: Harper & Row, 1970.

Rossi, P. H., Freeman, H. E., and Wright, S. R. *Evaluation: A Systematic Approach*. Newbury Park, Calif.: Sage, 1979.

Sedlacek, W. E., and Brooks, G. C., Jr. *Racism in American Education: A Model for Change*. Chicago: Nelson-Hall, 1976.

Stufflebeam, D. L., Foley, W. J., Gephart, W. J., Guba, E. G., Hammond, R. L., Merriman, R. L., and Provus, M. M. *Educational Evaluation and Decision Making*. Itasca, Ill.: Peacock, 1971.

Sudman, S., and Bradburn, N. M. *Asking Questions: A Practical Guide to Questionnaire Design*. San Francisco: Jossey-Bass, 1982.

Tracey, T. J., and Sedlacek, W. E. "Noncognitive Variables in Predicting Academic Success by Race." *Measurement and Evaluation in Guidance*, 1984, *16*, 171-178.

Tracey, T. J., and Sedlacek, W. E. "The Relationship of Noncognitive Variables to Academic Success: A Longitudinal Comparison by Race." *Journal of College Student Personnel*, 1985, *26*, 405-410.

Tracey, T. J., and Sedlacek, W. E. "Prediction of College Graduation Using Noncognitive Variables by Race." *Measurement and Evaluation in Counseling and Development*, 1987, *19*, 177-184.

White, T. J., and Sedlacek, W. E. "Noncognitive Predictors of Grades and Retention for Specially Admitted Students." *Journal of College Admissions*, 1986, *3*, 20-23.

William E. Sedlacek is assistant director of the Counseling Center at the University of Maryland. He has written widely on measurement and evaluation issues in student affairs, and is currently editor of Measurement and Evaluation in Counseling and Development.

An evaluation of a counseling center must examine its goals, activities, and impact and determine the balance among preventive, remedial, and developmental objectives.

Evaluating Counseling Centers

Robert D. Brown

Counseling centers exist on almost every campus, large and small, public and private. They provide services to help students with their educational, vocational, and personal development and are frequently staffed with professionally trained personnel, many with doctoral degrees in psychology or related fields. They are an important student service but, like all student services, are subject to intense scrutiny in this era of budget cuts and retrenchment. Tough questions must be asked: Is the counseling center needed? Are the staff doing their job? Are the staff as effective as they could be? Could the same services be provided more economically?

This chapter provides a framework for answering these and similar questions by describing an evaluation approach that can be used to conduct a formative self-assessment by the center staff (indeed, one criterion for a good center is that it is constantly engaged in self-evaluation activities), provide information for someone external to the center who must make programmatic and budgetary decisions affecting the counseling center, and evaluate other student services such as campus activities, financial aid, or residential education programs.

Three components comprise this evaluation framework: goal evaluation, activity evaluation, and impact evaluation (GAI). Three questions serve as the guide for determining the nature of the evaluation information collected: (1) What are the goals of the counseling center, and how are they determined and justified? (2) What does the staff do? and (3)

What is the impact of the center's activities? Although particular evaluation questions or purposes may focus on one or the other components of the GAI approach, all components must be considered as they are highly interactive. If the evaluation is formative and designed to help improve the counseling center, the focus might be primarily on activity evaluation, but the activities must be compared to the goals. A summative evaluation might emphasize goal and impact evaluation.

The rest of this chapter describes each component of the GAI approach, illustrates questions the evaluation might try to answer, and provides examples of information that could be collected.

Goal Evaluation: What Are the Goals and Are They Appropriate?

The first question asked in many evaluations is, "What are your goals?" When this is answered, too often the next step is to devise an evaluation to assess how well the agency has accomplished its goals. The first step in an evaluation, however, should be to evaluate the worth of the goals; this is particularly true when evaluating a student service. Suppose a counseling center decides to spend a significant share of its time and resources improving the academic and personal adjustment of student-athletes. As a result of this effort, the college's athletes graduate at a dramatically higher rate than athletes at comparable colleges. According to this criterion, the staff have achieved their goal. But at what expense? Perhaps the attrition rate for other students is dramatically higher than for comparable institutions. Or, perhaps students have to wait seven to ten days before they can see a counselor for a problem or decision that demands resolution in a shorter time.

A counseling center staff may do an exceptional job of achieving their objectives, but these may not be congruent with institutional philosophy or responsive to student needs. The worth of goals of the counseling center must be evaluated, the appropriateness of the balance among the goals considered, and the resources to meet the goals assessed.

Evaluating the Worth of the Goals. The first step in assessing goals is determining how many of the stated goals fall into the following three categories: preventive, remedial, and developmental. College counselors have served traditionally in remedial roles. They assist students experiencing academic trouble, career indecision, or emotional problems. Many other student services also serve in remedial roles. These are important responsibilities, but student services and counseling centers can and should also serve in preventive and developmental roles (Morrill, Oetting, and Hurst, 1974). The counseling center staff should not wait for students to come to their offices with problems and crises; the staff need to be working to prevent problems and to help students fulfill their potential for personal development (Brown, 1980b). Health and medical professionals provide outreach educational programs on preventive medicine and wellness. Most student health centers now see educational efforts on alcohol, drugs, AIDS, and other concerns as important missions. We must expect the same from campus counseling centers and other student services.

Determining the Balance Among Goals and Specific Worth. The next step is to determine the adequacy of the balance among the goals and the worth of the specific goals within each category. Should the goals be balanced equally among the three approaches or should one category be primary? How do we determine the worth of specific goals within each category?

Assessment of the worth of specific goals and their relative importance must be done at the institutional level and necessitates a needs assessment (Corazzini, 1979) and a match-up of institutional goals and resources. Almost any student issue or problem has potential implications for student services and counseling centers in particular. Needs assessments must be conducted from multiple perspectives (Scriven, 1980). It is important to look at the developmental needs of all students as well as the crisis needs of students involved in drugs, facing career indecision, or failing courses. These crises are important, but it is essential that they do not blind student services staff or the institution to the needs of all students.

Determining the Resources Available. Three questions must be asked about resources: (1) What are staff competencies? (2) What are the physical and financial resources? and (3) How much time is available? These questions are highly interactive, and the answers must be related to institutional goals and needs. Counseling center staff are often judged competent on the basis of their clinical skills, usually in one-to-one counseling. Can they deal with the severely disturbed? Can they administer and interpret sophisticated psychological assessment devices? These are important skills, but staff resources could be highly limited if these are the primary or sole criteria. An evaluation must ask, How well can the staff do group counseling, train other staff, and work with faculty? If staff competencies consist primarily of providing individual psychotherapy, then the remedial needs of emotionally disturbed students are likely to be the primary focus to the exclusion of the preventive and developmental programs. The skills of the staff must match those of the goals of the center, and these must be broad enough to respond to preventive and developmental, as well as remedial, needs. This does not mean that all staff must function equally well in all service activities, but it is important that the staff have the necessary skills and interests.

Financial, physical, and time resources must also be matched with the center's goals and the constraints of limited resources noted. Most counseling centers will have to set priorities. It might be helpful to examine the center's long-range plans as well as its immediate activities. Do the staff plan to phase in programs and other intervention strategies to meet student and institutional needs? Do they have a plan indicating how they would use additional staff?

Activity Evaluation: What Does the Counseling Center Do?

Two dimensions must be considered when evaluating the activities of the counseling center staff. First, a descriptive profile of activities must be made and matched with the center's goals. Second, the outcomes of these activities must be assessed.

Activity Profile

An evaluation must look carefully at who does what and for whom. "Who" refers to the staff, and may include peer counselors, paraprofessionals, or interns as well as counseling center staff. "What" refers to the activities, and "whom" to whether or not the activities are targeted for students or for others who work with students (for example, faculty or residence hall staff).

The preventive, remedial, and developmental framework can also be used for examining the relevance of counseling center activities. What activities does the center perform that could be considered preventive? These might include a workshop on time and stress management for residence hall students or a career decision-making session as part of a new-student orientation. Remedial activities might include one-to-one counseling with emotionally disturbed students and a reading skills improvement course for students on academic probation. Developmental programming might include involvement in planning wellness or multicultural awareness programs.

A counseling center that provides only direct services to individual students is perhaps performing a useful service for those students but is doing a disservice to other students because of the failure to effectively enhance the educational climate for all students. To have an impact on all students within budget, staff, and time constraints means improving the campus environment through contacts with others who educate students (Banning, 1980). Thus, the "for whom" component must include other audiences such as faculty, student affairs staff, parents, and other staff members. These audiences can be categorized as primary groups (for example, families, couples, friends), associational groups (for example, clubs, student government, residence hall groups), and institutional groups (for example, administrators, faculty) (Morrill, Oetting, and Hurst, 1974).

Activities targeted for the primary group might include sessions during orientation that help parents understand the adjustments their sons or daughters will have to make when they arrive on campus or efforts to sensitize students through campus newspaper articles on the signs of severe depression. The primary group remains a major resource and often the first resource for students when they need help. These persons continue to play an influential role in the development of college students (Stonewater, Stonewater, and Allen, 1983).

Student life can be influenced positively or negatively by the associational group. Working with student leaders provides them with developmental experiences as well as support for their efforts. That could have a positive impact on the campus climate. Attention to racial issues, for example, could raise the quality of life for ethnic minorities on campus. Other student service agencies (for example, campus activities) should also be involved with associational groups, but counseling center staff can provide expertise for workshops, presentations, or ideas for specific skill training (for example, listening skills).

Another important audience for counseling center staff might be institutional groups such as other campus agencies, faculty, and administrators. Counseling center staff might work with the financial aid staff to heighten their awareness of the opportunities to provide educational and developmental experiences for students who are striving for financial independence and need help in planning budgets. Faculty might be informed of ways they could help prevent or alleviate test anxiety. Administrators might be consulted on different policies to deal with AIDS.

Comparing the activities that take up the time of a counseling center staff to their stated goals is an excellent way for the staff to engage in formative evaluation and for an external decision maker to match the rhetoric of goal statements with the reality of a center's activities. Each activity can be matched with its appropriate goal or goals. The number of staff and the amount of staff time allotted to each activity can be noted. If the goals have been arranged by their priority, the comparisons can be straightforward. It will be possible to note, for example, that Goal A was considered to be 20 percent of the center's focus, but has 40 percent of the staff working on it with 60 percent of their time. On the other hand, Goal B was considered to be 40 percent of the center's focus but has only 15 percent of the staff assigned to it only 10 percent of their time. Such misalignments of priorities and staff time may be appropriate if events have warranted a change. The comparison, however, makes the staff and planners aware of the need to reexamine priorities and perhaps their activities.

Activities Outcomes

Three activities outcomes are important to assess: (1) the number, kind, and length of student contacts, (2) number and kind of contacts with other staff and faculty, and (3) perceptions of roles and usefulness by other staff, faculty, and students. These outcomes should be compared for their congruency with the counseling center goals and the center staff's activities.

Student Contacts. The nature of the services provided to students and the number of students served can indicate how well the center is fulfilling goals related to preventive, remedial, and developmental activities. It is helpful to know key characteristics of these students as well as the number served. Were the students who came to the life-planning workshop freshmen or juniors? Were they students "at risk" or were they "A" students? What kind of students come to the center for vocational counseling—are there more men than women, more from the sciences than the arts, more of the brighter than the less bright students? Knowing the average range of contacts the staff have with individual students is also helpful. How many students are seen for what might be considered long-term therapy, and is this appropriate? It might be appropriate for some staff members to carry a few long-term clients for self-development or training purposes, but is the balance appropriate?

Faculty and Staff Contacts. The kinds of contacts with faculty and other staff provide a helpful index of the relationship of the counseling center to others on campus. Are there formal or informal liaisons with colleges or departments? Does the staff consult with faculty on advising programs? Are the staff involved in planning and implementing new-student orientation programs, residence education programs, or special task forces to study the curriculum or the campus environment? What is the extent of the staff's involvement in programs for parents, high school counselors, and others? These kinds of contacts should be as much a part of the evaluation data of a counseling center as the data related to direct contact with students.

Role Perceptions and Expectations. How do the staff view their role? Do they see themselves as educators, being involved with the total campus, concerned about the typical student as well as the academically at risk and the emotionally unsettled? Equally important is how others see the counseling center. Do students see the center primarily as a place for "sick" students to go? (This is an image that many students have despite the best efforts of counseling centers.) Do faculty consult with staff on matters other than how to refer students? If the faculty were designing a new course to help freshmen adjust to college, would they invite the counseling center staff to be involved? Also important is what campus administrators think about the counseling center. Are they aware that the center has the potential for affecting the entire campus population, that the center does not work with just the emotionally disturbed or the academically "at risk" students?

These outcomes are necessary if other student and campus outcomes are to be achieved. Collecting information about these outcomes provides indices of how well the center is fulfilling its goals and how appropriate its activities are. No matter what the goals and activities are, if students and faculty see the center as solely a place for emotionally disturbed students and career-undecided students, the potential impact of the center is limited. If staff are spending an inordinate amount of time in one-to-one contact with emotionally disturbed students when they profess to be interested in developmental concerns of all students, this incongruency can be discussed.

Impact Evaluation: What Impact Does the Center Have?

Many administrators concentrate evaluation efforts on the ultimate or "bottom line" impact of a counseling center—how are students helped and how does this relate to graduation rate and retention? This emphasis, however, can be shortsighted. If the evaluation focuses exclusively on the final impact, it is highly unlikely that the information will provide helpful clues about what must be done differently. If the evaluation does not look at the goals, activities, and outcomes of the activities, these dimensions remain mysterious black boxes, and the chances for helpful insights on how to improve services will range from minimal to nonexistent. It is essential that an evaluation plan be ongoing, not an occasional event, and that the evaluation focus on all the dimensions, including goals and processes as well as impact.

Counseling centers are typically remiss in collecting these "bottom-line" data. Counseling centers can readily determine how many students they saw for certain kinds of problems, and information about preventive and remedial activities is or should be readily available. Although it is more difficult to find out how many students resolved emotional issues or advanced further on a developmental scale, counseling centers, like their academic counterparts in higher education who are being asked for more student outcome data, should provide data demonstrating their impact on students and on other dimensions of campus life.

With these perspectives in mind, let us consider several important indices of impact: (1) student and faculty satisfaction, (2) differences between clients and nonclients, (3) campus climate assessments, and (4) cost-outcome analyses.

Student Satisfaction and Self-Assessment. Counseling centers collect data on student satisfaction with their services. These measures should include feedback on components of the services such as how they heard about the service, what they expected, how they were treated in the reception-intake process, what their perceptions were of the counselor's interest and help, how they believed they have changed, and whether they have ideas for improvement and would recommend the service to others. This information should be collected routinely from at least a representative sample. Summaries by year or semester should be available.

Differences Between Clients and Nonclients. It is difficult for student services to conduct rigorous experiments that involve random sampling because their clientele is self-selected (Brown, 1980a). Ethical and political issues make it difficult for centers to randomly provide services for some students but withhold them from others for purposes of having a control group. It might happen, however, that more students express an interest in the center's group efforts on decision making or test anxiety workshops than there is room for—perhaps forty students express an interest but only twenty can be accommodated. The twenty students could be selected randomly to be included in the first round and the rest put into a delayed treatment program. Both groups could be tested and compared at the end of the treatment period.

When the possibilities of a random control group cohort are slim, staff should be encouraged to look at alternatives such as matched comparison groups and comparing two forms of delivering the same service. The key evaluation question is often not whether a career decision-making workshop is helpful, but which format for a workshop is most effective. Asking these kinds of questions, as well as systematically obtaining expected feedback on student satisfication, should be part of an ongoing evaluation program.

Campus Climate Assessment. It is unfair to expect that the counseling center by itself is going to change dramatically the attitudes of faculty toward students, of students toward the institution, or of students toward learning. It is not unreasonable, however, for the center to be involved in that process. Considering the typical center's budget and staff limitation, it is more realistic to expect the staff to be involved in three efforts to improve the campus climate: (1) assessing campus needs, (2) helping the campus community to interpret and respond to those needs, and (3) being involved in addressing some of the needs themselves.

Cost-Outcome Analysis. Putting a dollar value on services is difficult for any human services agency, and it is particularly difficult for educators and for those providing student services. Academic departments can count the credit hours or graduates and use that figure as the denominator of an equation that has costs as the numerator. But how do you put dollar values on emotional adjustment, better study skills, or enhanced human development? Some form of cost-outcome analysis, however, should be an integral part of the evaluation of student services because the analyses can be helpful in making program decisions as well as providing information in a form that will be useful to other campus administrators and decision makers.

Two forms of cost-outcome analysis are appropriate for making decisions about counseling centers: cost-effectiveness ratios and cost-benefit ratios. Brief definitions and examples of how these might be used in the evaluation of counseling centers follow.

Cost-effectiveness analyses compare the costs of programs with outcomes expressed as standard units (for example, test scores, grade-point averages, number of students graduated) (Levin, 1983). Unfortunately, too many people forget that cost-effectiveness is intended for comparative purposes by using indices of quality as well as simply the number of students served. They think that a report that shows an agency spending less this year than last means the agency is more cost-effective. This is not necessarily the case because it is likely that, besides spending less, the agency also provided fewer services. So it is important for those preparing cost information and for those making decisions to complete the ratio and to do so comparatively.

If number of students served is the unit, then providing group counseling for students is certainly more cost-effective than providing one-to-one counseling for students. In this case, the ratio would be the staff salary and related costs divided by the number of students served. A half-time counselor (for example, salary $15,000) seeing 75 students individually during an academic year yields a cost-effective ratio of $200.00 per student. The same counselor seeing 150 students in small groups during the academic year yields a cost-effective ratio of $100.00 per student. Unfortunately, this approach considers only the number of students seen, not the quality of the services or the impact on students. Measures of quality might be scores on a career maturity inventory or number of students making a solid career decision. Using these measures in the cost-effectiveness ratio analysis may result in a different conclusion. Suppose the half-time counselor's 75 individually seen students all moved one year ahead in career maturity while the half-time counselor who saw 150 students only moved .33 year ahead in career maturity. The cost-effectiveness of the one-to-one counselor would be $200 per year to career maturity ($15,000 salary/75 career maturity years = $200), whereas the cost-effectiveness for the group counselor would be $303 per year of career maturity [$15,000 salary/(.33 × 150 students) = $303].

This example demonstrates the importance of determining what the standard unit should be (grades, retention figures, improved satisfaction scores). It is most appropriately used for evaluative decision making when the ratios compare the relative costs of providing the same services and look at the quality or impact of those services, not just the number of persons served.

Cost-benefit analysis compares the outcomes of programs as measured in dollar amounts and is an approach that can be used when programs have different objectives (Thompson, 1980). The cost-effectiveness example compared programs that had the same objective—improved career maturity scores. Suppose we wanted to compare the career development group program to a test anxiety workshop? These programs have different objectives, so comparing costs on number of students served or on objective assessment of career maturity scores and test anxiety scores is not appropriate. For this comparison we have to make a judgment about the relative worth of the benefits. A cost-benefit analysis attempts to do this by making the dollar the common comparison unit. What is the dollar value that can be assigned to a year of career maturity or to test-taking skills? This is not an easy task. Besides considering the dollar value of career maturity or test-taking skills in isolation, the judgment must also consider supplementary benefits such as satisfaction with college, likelihood of staying in college, benefits of correct career choice, or considerations of improved grades. Benefits might be examined from the perspective of those accruing to the student or those accruing to the institution.

Although the analysis seems complex and perhaps overwhelming, it is important to remember that judgments like these are being made by one method or another whenever budget decisions are made. The cost-benefit approach is an attempt to use common units to make the value judgments when someone decides to drop a program or put more emphasis on one program than another. When counseling centers decide to change or drop test anxiety programs or to put more emphasis on career development than on relaxation workshops, they are making the same judgment, but it may be based on the staff's intuition, personal preferences, or political pressure. Such sources are important, but the cost-benefit approach can be useful for providing a framework for thinking of outcomes and their relative worth for the student and the institution.

Cost-outcome analyses can no longer be avoided. The approach does not remove value judgments nor does it necessarily let numbers or dollar signs rule. Indeed, cost-outcome approaches can force us to think concretely about the worth of the services provided to students.

Conclusion

This chapter presented a framework for administrators who want to evaluate counseling centers. The GAI framework (summarized in Figure 1), combined with looking for the balance among preventive, remedial, and developmental efforts, can be useful for an external evaluator looking at the activities and effectiveness of other student services as well as the counseling center. The same questions apply: Are the goals appropriately balanced among preventive, remedial, and developmental objectives? Do the programs match the goals? What happens in the programs, and are the programs effective in achieving their goals? The same perspectives can be used by counseling centers or directors of other student services to design an ongoing self-evaluation program for formative purposes.

Figure 1. Goal, Activity, and Impact Evaluation of a College Counseling Center

Goal Evaluation

1. Are preventive and developmental goals included as well as remedial ones?
2. Is the balance among the remedial, preventive, and developmental goals congruent with institutional goals?
3. Are resources (time, money, space) appropriately allocated to the goals?

Activity Evaluation

1. Who provides services for students (for example, level of training/background)?
2. What activities are engaged in by the counseling center staff?
3. Do the activities match the stated goals of the counseling center?
4. How are the services delivered (for example, group, individual)?
5. Who are the targeted groups for services and programs (for example, students, friends, parents, faculty)?
6. What are the characteristics of students who are provided services, and what services are provided?
7. What are the characteristics of contacts with faculty and others?
8. What are the perceptions of roles and usefulness by students, faculty, and administrators?

Impact Evaluation

1. How satisfied are students and others with services, consultation, and programs?
2. What evidence is there that students are positively influenced by the services and programs?
3. What evidence is there that the campus environment has been influenced by the services and programs?
4. How cost-effective are the services and programs?

The goal of the evaluation must be to provide the best services possible for the students within agency and institutional constraints. Evaluation is always a challenge, but if conducted in an atmosphere conducive to honest inquiry and self-examination, it can be intellectually stimulating and rewarding. Evaluation can be a useful tool for improving student services and result in direct benefits to students.

References

Banning, J. "The Campus Ecology Manager Role." In U. Delworth, G. R. Hanson, and Associates (eds.), *Student Services: A Handbook for the Profession.* San Francisco: Jossey-Bass, 1980.

Brown, R. D. "Evaluating Campus Learning Centers." In O. T. Lenning and R. L. Nayman (eds.), *New Roles for Learning Assistance.* New Directions for College Learning Assistance, no. 2. San Francisco: Jossey-Bass, 1980a.

Brown, R. D. "The Student Development Educator Role." In U. Delworth, G. R. Hanson, and Associates (eds.), *Student Services: A Handbook for the Profession.* San Francisco: Jossey-Bass, 1980b.

Corazzini, J. G. "Counseling Center." In G. D. Kuh (ed.), *Evaluation in Student Affairs.* Cincinnati, Ohio: American College Personnel Association, 1979.

Levin, H. *Cost-Effectiveness: A Primer.* Newbury Park, Calif.: Sage Publications, 1983.

Morrill, W. H., Oetting, E. R., and Hurst, J. C. "Dimensions of Counseling Functioning." *Personnel and Guidance Journal,* 1974, *52,* 354–359.

Scriven, M. *Evaluation Thesaurus.* Pt. Reyes, Calif.: Edgepress, 1981.

Stonewater, B. B., Stonewater, J. K., and Allen, T. R. "Using Developmental Theory in a Parent's Orientation Session." *Journal of College Student Personnel,* 1983, *24,* 455–456.

Thompson, M. *Benefit-Cost Analysis for Program Evaluation.* Newbury Park, Calif.: Sage Publications, 1980.

Robert D. Brown is assistant dean for research and evaluation and professor of educational psychology at Teachers College, University of Nebraska, Lincoln. He has published extensively on college student development and on utilization of evaluation information. He is editor of the Journal of College Student Personnel.

The future of faculty development programs will benefit most from a systematic assessment of program goals.

Evaluating Faculty Development Programs: Program Goals First

Robert E. Young

"If the goals [of a program] aren't worth achieving, then it is uninteresting to know how well they are achieved" (Scriven, 1967, p. 40). These may be the most unattended words in the short history of program evaluation. They are particularly important words for faculty development programs and their evaluation.

Most evaluators of programs in higher education take program goals for granted and instead focus their methods on describing with as much precision as possible the process and products of the program. Few examples can be identified that systematically look at program goals in advance of implementing and assessing a program. This chapter poses a new emphasis for the evaluation of faculty development programs.

Faculty development programs continue to be a growth industry in American higher education. After a predicted decline of programs to improve college and university teaching (Sullivan, 1983), we find ourselves at a time of even greater interest and activity (Eble and McKeachie, 1985; Erickson, 1986). During the past five years a number of major universities and a myriad of small colleges have begun new programs or have rejuvenated existing programs. Foundations, most notably the Bush and Ford foundations and the Lilly Endowment, have recently made major commitments to faculty development. The interest in faculty development stands only to gain steam with the current attention to undergraduate education (National Institute of Education, 1985; Association of American Colleges, 1985; Boyer, 1987).

Historically, faculty development programs have been collections of institution-wide resources to assist faculty members as they pursue their responsibilities of teaching, research, and service. In the past twenty years many of the new developments and programs have focused on teaching. In fact, faculty development (unfortunately) has become synonymous with the improvement of college teaching. With this focus on teaching, the resources of faculty development programs typically include people (sometimes experienced faculty members and sometimes specialists) who consult with faculty members about teaching problems and projects; money for development and experimentation; technologies that might include facilities and equipment; and services, such as test scoring and course evaluation. A hallmark of the faculty development movement of the past two decades has been the variety of approaches that campuses have taken.

Just as faculty development programs have gotten much attention, so has the evaluation of these programs. Gaff (1975, p. 4), in his seminal book on faculty development programs, argued that "Unless we evaluate our programs and demonstrate that they produce results . . . we will be out of business." Wergin (1977) observed, "Now, perhaps, the movement is ready for . . . reflection on its assumptions, processes, and effects" (p. 58).

Yet, evaluation continues to be a self-conscious side of the faculty development movement. Kenneth Eble and Wilbert McKeachie, long-time observers of faculty development programs, have recently echoed the belief of most people in the field: "Evaluation of faculty development programs is difficult. While most . . . are intended to help faculty members become more effective teachers and scholars, obtaining convincing evidence of these effects is rare" (Eble and McKeachie, 1985, p. 177). For ten years there has been similar dissatisfaction about the results of faculty development programs and how to prove their worth and effectiveness.

Much of the consternation is justified. We need new, more sophisticated methods of evaluating the results of programs in higher education. The thesis of this chapter is that one aspect of evaluation is most critical—the clarity and fidelity of the goals of a faculty development program. When looking at goals, the concern is not whether a program accomplishes what it intends, that is, whether it meets its objectives or whether there is congruence between its goals and its attainments, but whether what is intended is worthwhile.

Eble and McKeachie (1985) conclude from their studies that "The most obvious and most refractory problem in evaluating faculty development programs is that of criteria." Wergin (1977) points out that faculty development programs, unlike other university programs, shoulder a special burden of proof: "It is hard to imagine similar 'show me' attitudes being held toward the registrar or office of student affairs" (p. 58). Not all faculty development programs find themselves in this position, but if Wergin is right about most programs, then this is all the more reason to be clear about goals. Again, Eble and McKeachie (1985, p. 78) observe that ". . . a single faculty development program is likely to produce only a dot on the mosaic of student experience." If this is true, then we should be careful about how we choose our priorities.

Most of the literature on the evaluation of faculty development programs has called for the evaluation of goals in the process of evaluation, and some of these statements have been very helpful, but little evidence exists that programs have given much attention to this step. A review of the faculty development literature reveals no reports of this type of evaluation. There are reports of faculty and student surveys, case studies, and even quasi-experiments, but none that portrays the evaluation of the goals of a faculty development program. The rest of this chapter proposes such an evaluation.

A Goals Evaluation

A goals evaluation can be organized around three questions: "Why do it? For whom should it be done? and How can it be accomplished?" These questions of reasons, audience, and design usually guide the planning of any successful evaluation. Let us consider each of these questions, building an approach to evaluating a faculty development program, and, since few examples exist, let me create a case study to exemplify how a campus might perform an evaluation of the goals of its faculty development program. The case might be thought of as a proposal from the chairperson of the faculty development committee at the "University of the North" (U. of N.) to the university senate and chief academic officer of the university. The case is a hypothetical one, but it represents an amalgam of thinking and experience about program evaluation in faculty development.

Reasons for the Evaluation

There might be many reasons for looking closely at the goals of a faculty development program. A campus may be just beginning a program, possibly by merging or reconstituting existing, small-scale programs. It has not been unusual for traditional media centers, with their particular set of goals, to be asked to take on a broader faculty development program. On the other hand, a campus might find itself in financial difficulty with the need to eliminate some of its programs; a goals evaluation can provide a way to determine the importance and priority of a faculty development program.

The faculty development program has existed at the University of the North since 1980. Its purpose, broadly stated, has been to improve the quality of instruction on the campus. Its activities have been aimed at assisting faculty and staff develop more effective and efficient instructional procedures. To accomplish this purpose, the program has prepared a set of goals and current objectives (Figure 1). But events have occurred recently that suggest that the program's goals merit a systematic reassessment.

Figure 1. Goals and Objectives at University of the North

Goals	Objectives[a]
Provide direct service to faculty members through materials, consultation, and assistance	Establish and maintain a library of print and audiovisual materials related to college teaching
	Increase the number of faculty members who engage in a formal, systematic evaluation of their teaching
	Participate with a small number of faculty groups in the development of exemplary instructional approaches and materials
Provide funds to support instruction development projects initiated by U. of N. faculty members and academic units	Increase faculty understanding of the opportunities for funding both on and off campus instructional development
	Offer special funding programs in areas of high need in the university, for example, writing instruction, instructional computing, values development
Serve as advocate for the improvement of instruction at U. of N.	Advise the executive officers and faculty committees regarding the improvement of instruction
	Strengthen existing instructional development services
	Seek additional resources for faculty development at U. of N.

[a] Each of these objectives would be followed by operating procedures designed to accomplish the objective.

The program has seen its staff and functional responsibilities expand considerably. The new personnel and set of functions have resulted in new and different ideas of how to approach the major purpose of the program—improving the quality of instruction at U. of N.

At the time the program was established, a small number of other universities were also creating campus agencies to coordinate instructional improvement, and a second generation of programs proliferated across the country. These programs have pursued a variety of goals (Figure 2). With this the case, it may be advantageous for the U. of N. faculty development program to evaluate itself against the experience of these other programs.

Other campuses might be doing sophisticated things, but our university has its own particular mission, student body, faculty, and culture. Although relatively stable in its purposes and organization, the university does experience some ebb and flow, and the faculty development program needs to continually adjust itself to these fluctuations. Program adminis-

Figure 2. Goals at Other Colleges and Universities

Wheatland University	*Fort Union State University*	*Pembina College*
Improve the intellectual atmosphere of the campus	Assist faculty members to develop in their disciplines	Increase understanding of students' interests, values, capabilities, and learning styles
Improve the classroom performance of faculty members	Increase interaction of faculty members with research scholars elsewhere, and provide faculty members and students with more extended contact with distinguished visiting scholars	Incorporate into the curriculum issues related to women and minorities
Increase the advising skills of faculty members		Increase interdisciplinary communication and integration of learning among faculty members
Provide curriculum development opportunities that go beyond usual course revisions and updating		Enhance the ability of faculty to teach writing in their disciplines
Assist departments in assessing their academic programs	Expand faculty experience in their fields outside of the academic setting	
	Identify and encourage creativity in students	
	Encourage research that accentuates the role of faculty members and students as practitioners of the liberal arts	

trators and staff have tried to be keen observers of the university, but its periodic shifts are not always immediately perceptible without a more systematic analysis. This is a third reason for a goals evaluation for the U. of N. faculty development program.

A fourth and final reason relates to the broader issue of program evaluation. As typically conceptualized, evaluation cannot proceed until the goals and current objectives of the program are clearly defined. Yet, the goals and objectives of a program must be considered worthy before it makes much sense to judge its results. The faculty development program has regularly collected data on the number of faculty members served, the changes effected in the curriculum and in faculty members' approach to their teaching, and (to a more limited degree) the impacts on students' learning. What is not known is whether the participation, projects, and impacts are the most important in terms of the existing purposes of the program and its capabilities, its internal resources, the characteristics of the university, and the experiences of similar programs at other universities.

Audience for the Evaluation

To whom is a goals evaluation directed? Who will be served by such an effort? As already implied, the results of this kind of evaluation are directed primarily at decision makers concerned with the operation of a faculty development program. The ultimate purpose of any goals analysis is to facilitate more rational planning and allocation of resources.

At U. of N. those administrators and committees within the university who have supervisory and budgeting responsibilities for the faculty development program have been involved in planning this goals evaluation. The academic vice president—to whom the program reports—and the senate-appointed faculty development committee will be the principal audiences for this evaluation. But the president, the individual college deans, administrative budget officers, and faculty steering and budget committees must be considered audiences as well.

The faculty development program itself will be able to use the information gathered to chart the future directions of the program, and to gauge its activities and performance against the goals identified.

Also, the faculty will benefit. Results disseminated within the university community will allow faculty to make determinations of whether and how the program might assist them with their instructional responsibilities. Finally, interested persons at other institutions (including administrators, faculty members, and faculty development staff) may find the results useful in planning and evaluating their own faculty development program.

Design of the Evaluation

A faculty development program, if it is to be successful, must state which goals are worth accomplishing. The development of this statement involves making a set of decisions that require data from a number of sources. The design of a goals evaluation (Figure 3) offers procedures for gathering and integrating information so that certain decisions can be made about the goals of a faculty development program.

Decisions. The principal outcome of this evaluation is the development of a statement of program goals. A useful statement should assess the worth of each potential goal, establish priorities for the goals considered worthwhile, and set a standard for the achievement of each goal. These issues define the decisions that are the focus of a goals evaluation and for which information needs to be gathered and integrated.

The goals evaluation proposed at the U. of N. poses these questions:

1. What is the worth of each possible goal for the program? This decision can be made by answering three related subquestions: (1) Is it related to the needs of the university, its students, and faculty members? (2) Is it feasible within the constraints imposed by the university and the program itself? and (3) Does it reflect what relevant groups and individuals think the program should be doing? These are the criteria for determining the worth of program goals and objectives.

2. How do these goals rank in importance? The goals' relative importance can be determined by looking at the resources and constraints imposed by the university and the program, the objective needs of the university, and the opinions of campus leaders.

3. What constitutes the standard of accomplishment for each goal or objective? Again, standards of achievement can be determined by the requirements of the university, its inputs and barriers, and the values of relevant groups and individuals.

Information Gathering. Figure 3 depicts the sources and nature of the information that must be collected in this form of goals evaluation. As the figure indicates, these data serve as input into the decisions described in the previous section.

Four categories of information merit consideration: the nature of the university in which the program operates, the characteristics of the program itself, the characteristics and needs of the "clients" whom the program serves, and the opinions of people who might have some influence on or interest in the program. As suggested above, the worth, priority, and standard of a goal depends on the resources and constraints of the university, the capabilities of the program, the needs and characteristics of the faculty and students, and the beliefs of certain important individuals and groups.

Figure 3. Design for Goals Evaluation at "University of the North"

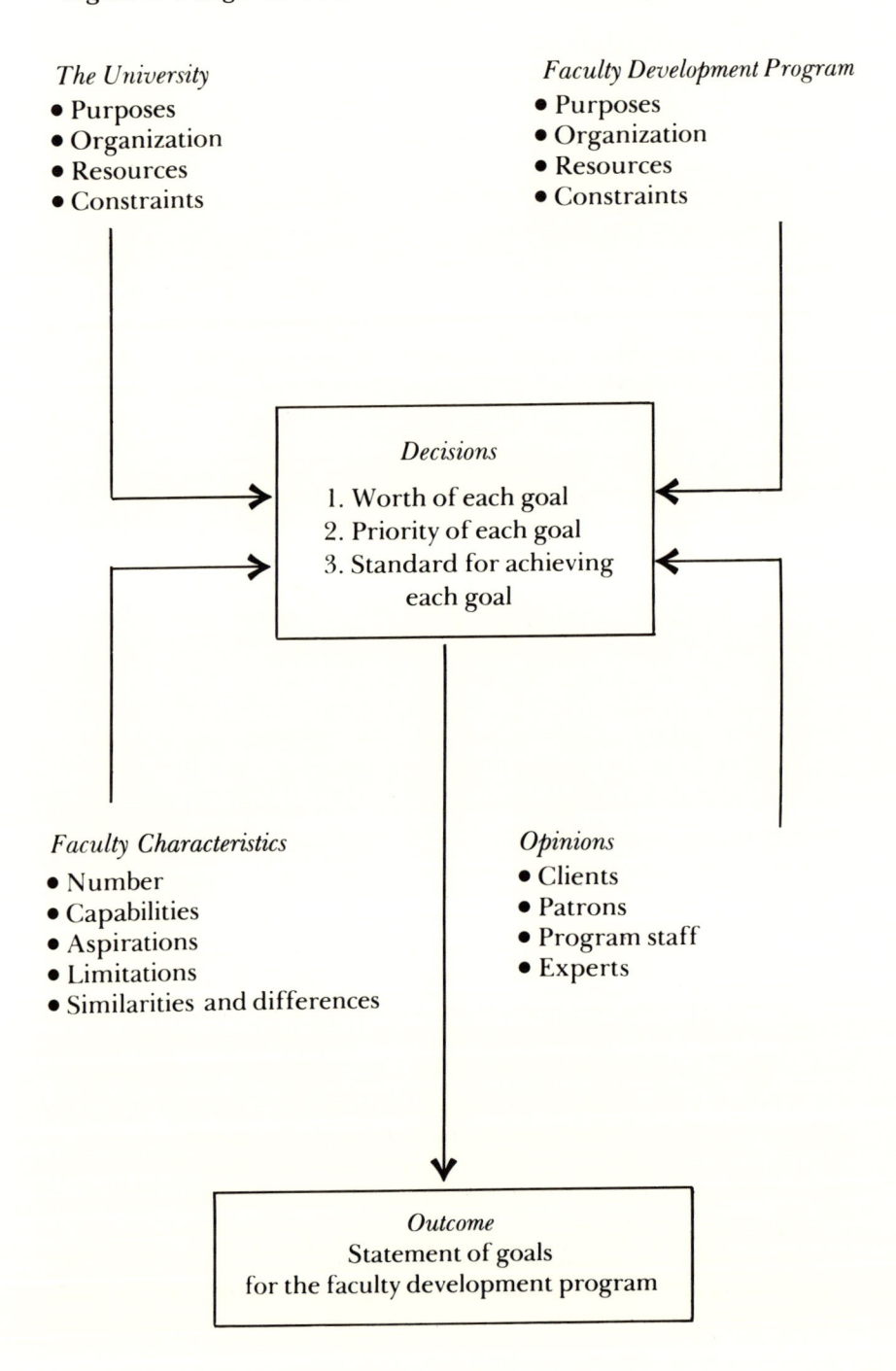

The University
- Purposes
- Organization
- Resources
- Constraints

Faculty Development Program
- Purposes
- Organization
- Resources
- Constraints

Decisions
1. Worth of each goal
2. Priority of each goal
3. Standard for achieving each goal

Faculty Characteristics
- Number
- Capabilities
- Aspirations
- Limitations
- Similarities and differences

Opinions
- Clients
- Patrons
- Program staff
- Experts

Outcome
Statement of goals for the faculty development program

This proposal suggests that the goals evaluation of the faculty development program be undertaken by a task force of faculty and staff, chaired by the chairperson of the faculty development committee. For the purposes of gathering information, the task force would be divided into four subgroups, and each would collect and summarize information from a particular source of information.

The first two groups would prepare a thorough description of the university and the existing faculty development program. The characteristics of the university and the capabilities of the program itself set parameters that the intents of a program cannot usually exceed without some change in the system.

In preparing a description of the university, dimensions relevant to the operation of the program must be investigated. The focus will be on the resources made available by the university to support directly or indirectly the activities of the program and the constraints that might preclude these activities. Specifically, information will be gathered on purposes, organization, resources (personnel, funding, materials and equipment, and facilities), and constraints. Data will be gathered primarily through an examination of existing documents and interviews with appropriate university personnel.

The description of the program will focus on the capabilities of the existing faculty development program, which will determine, in part, the range of goals possible for the program. Specifically, information will be gathered on the purposes, organization, resources, and constraints within the program. This description will be based on a review of existing documents and a survey of program personnel focused on determining individual and group capabilities.

A third subgroup will gather information on client characteristics and needs, that is, a description of the faculty and academic staff of the university. The instructional needs of individuals and groups of faculty and staff indicate where the faculty development program might be most useful. Whereas the characteristics of the program and the larger university set limits for the program's activities, the needs and characteristics of the client population provide a view of what could be the outcomes of the program.

Data on client characteristics and needs can be collected by a sample survey of university faculty and academic staff members by using standard needs analysis procedures. Specifically, information will be gathered on who the clients are, their number, skills, backgrounds, aspirations, and how they are different from and similar to each other.

A fourth subgroup would investigate what important individuals and groups think the goals of the program should be. Program staff and administrators responsible for supervision and operation of the program, clients, and experts inside and outside the university all have opinions about how the program should function. Wergin (1977) reminds us that faculty development programs exist in a world of judges, each with his or her own implicit standards for the program.

These opinions will be gathered by separate surveys or interviews of these groups and individuals. For some groups, all members will be questioned; for others, only a sample will be asked to respond. Expert opinion will be sought from on and off campus, other programs will be observed for their goals and objectives, and the faculty development literature will be consulted.

Each of the four subgroups will prepare a summary of their findings that must be cogent and economical. The data must be presented so that intended audiences can use them directly and, more important, so that this information can be used in the process of making decisions about the worth and priority of possible goals for the faculty development program.

Integration of Information. A goals evaluation intends as its final product a formal statement of goals. To produce such a statement, the evaluators must treat the information as input into a decision-making process and design a strategy for making decisions. The decision makers may prefer to provide their own integration of the data, either separate from or in addition to that produced by an evaluator or evaluation committee. With this in mind, the following strategy might guide the integration of information and the development of a statement of goals for a faculty development program.

The strategy represents a three-stage approach to assessing potential outcomes and selecting the single most valid set for a faculty development program. This approach, particularly at stage three, represents a model of organizational decision making that has been implicit throughout this description of a goals assessment.

This model holds that decisions about any program within a college or university are made through a series of progressive delimitations of the list of possible alternatives. As suggested earlier, the university sets parameters outside of which possible goals cannot be considered. In the case of a service organization, such as a faculty development program, the characteristics and needs of the client population further reduce the desirable and feasible set of program goals. Then, the capabilities of the program itself most probably eliminate additional possibilities. Finally, the influence of important groups and individuals, characterized by their beliefs on the proper functions of the program, will result in the set of alternatives that will most likely become the goals of the program.

At the U. of N., a possible strategy for employing the information gathered by the four subgroups into a single statement of program goals follows. First, a list of possible goals needs to be generated. Using all the information gathered and any other input available, the evaluation task force (and anyone else who will help out) will brainstorm all conceivable outcomes for a program that has as its mission the improvement of instruction. At this stage, attention should not be given to particular constraints or to the desirability or feasibility of a goal.

Then, the list of possible goals must be considered in light of the information collected about the university, program, clients, and subjective judges. These sources of data, considered in turn, will result in the acceptance of some of the possible goals and the rejection of others. This strategy actually results in four separate lists produced by testing the list of possible goals against each particular source of information.

The third and final stage involves putting these lists together into a single statement. Each list will be compared in a successive fashion with the next in line—in this case, university, clients, program, and judges. The process is as follows. Of the goals on the university list, those that also appear on the client statement are accepted and the rest rejected. These goals are then compared with the program list; those on both lists are accepted. Finally, these goals are matched with the list based on the opinions of important groups and individuals. The goals that survive this successive delimiting of possible goals represent the single most valid statement of goals for the faculty development program at the University of the North.

The University of the North is not atypical in the realm of faculty development programs. Many programs have been in place for some time, and a number of new, substantial programs are begun each year. These programs often find themselves under unusual scrutiny right from their beginnings. Evaluation is a fact of life for faculty development programs, even where evaluation has not been formal and systematic. Most faculty development programs and those to whom they answer collect data, even if only anecdotes and impressions, and decisions are made with these data. Clearly, evaluation of faculty development programs must become more sophisticated. Good models and examples have emerged over the past decade. But, first and foremost, it is the goals of a faculty development program and their worth to a college and university that need attention. Not only is it uninteresting to know how well faculty development programs succeed if their goals are not worth achieving, it may mean the difference in the real success and the very existence of faculty development programs in the near future.

References

Association of American Colleges. *Integrity in the College Curriculum.* Washington, D.C.: Association of American Colleges, 1985.

Boyer, E. *College: The Undergraduate Experience in America.* New York: Harper & Row, 1987.

Eble, K. E., and McKeachie, W. J. *Improving Undergraduate Education Through Faculty Development: An Analysis of Effective Programs and Practices.* San Francisco: Jossey-Bass, 1985.

Erickson, G. "A Survey of Faculty Development Practices." In M. Svinicki (ed.), *To Improve the Academy.* Kingston, R.I.: Professional and Organizational Development Network in Higher Education, 1986.

Gaff, J. G. *Toward Faculty Renewal: Advances in Faculty, Instructional, and Organizational Development.* San Francisco: Jossey-Bass, 1975.

National Institute of Education. *Involvement in Learning.* Report of the Study Group on the Conditions of Excellence in Higher Education. Washington, D.C.: National Institute of Education, 1985.

Scriven, M. "The Methodology of Evaluation." In R. W. Tyler, R. M. Gagne, and M. Scriven (eds.), *Perspectives on Curriculum Evaluation.* Skokie, Ill.: Rand McNally, 1967.

Sullivan, L. L. "Faculty Development: A Movement on the Brink." *The College Board Review,* no. 127, Spring 1983.

Wergin, J. F. "Evaluating Faculty Development Programs." In J. A. Centra (ed.), *Renewing and Evaluating Teaching.* New Directions for Higher Education, no. 5. San Francisco: Jossey-Bass, 1977.

Robert E. Young is dean, University of Wisconsin Center–Fox Valley. He formerly was director of the office of instructional development at the University of North Dakota.

The evaluation of campus computer services has been limited by the ability of higher education administrators to relate their experience in evaluating other, more traditional, services to the explosive growth and technical complexity of computing services.

Evaluating Campus Computing Services: Taming the Technology

Robert G. Gillespie

Evaluation of campus computing requires a clear vision of the purpose of the evaluation: Is it to be operational? Directed toward adequacy of response to its users? Identified with the planning direction? Pushed by profusion of personal computers? Linked to a change in role and goals for academic computing with respect to campus goals? Brought about by a change in the management of the center, or the university? Focused on the academic services? The academic center? The administrative computing?

Computing services on campus can be divided into services that support the academic community, services that support administrative functions, and those that overlap. Even though a single organization on campus may support both these functions, the evaluation planning will differ because the communities served are quite different. The goals and approaches are quite different: the administrative functions are usually highly centralized and computing services support the drive for integration of data bases that support student, financial, and development activities. With the technological opportunities brought about by the availability of personal computers, and because the users themselves are involved in the programming and development of computing services, academic computing requires a different, more decentralized approach.

The evaluation of any function has to involve weighing the goals and objectives against the resources and constraints. The expectations of the faculty, students, and administration must be weighed against the resources available. This chapter will describe planning for evaluation focusing on issues affecting computing evaluation, objectives and framework for the evaluation, components of an evaluation plan, some suggested criteria for evaluation, and the implementation of the results.

What Issues Are Affecting the Evaluation of Computing?

Some of the key issues affecting computing have been increases in the total cost of computing, the need for a strategy to deal with personal computers, and the pressures that force the development of integrated plans for campus communications.

Cost. In 1970, higher education spent approximately $500 million on computing, which was about equally split between administration, research, and instruction (Gillespie, 1983). In 1980, $1.3 billion was spent (out of $40 billion for higher education), with administration estimated at 50 percent. Since the National Science Foundation ceased its regular surveys, only estimates can be derived for current expenditure levels. According to Warlick (1986, p. A-7), the annual rate of growth for computing budgets has been approximately 15 percent since 1981, which means that current computing costs are over $2.6 billion. The most recent estimate for the average percentage of the institutional budget that is spent on computing (academic computing center and administrative computing) is 3 percent. Since much of the growth in computing expenditures is taking place in departmental budgets rather than in computing budgets, due to the purchases of personal computers and workstations, we can assume even larger amounts may be spent on computing—as much as 5 to 10 percent of the budget at many institutions. If the definition is broadened from computing to information services, thus including the library, reproduction, printing, and communications services, the campus percentage of the budget is even higher.

Personal Computer Strategy. Personal computers are rapidly penetrating the institutions for use as word processors (Levine, Strenta, and Wolford, 1986). However, each campus finds it necessary to develop its own strategy for this new information tool. Some of the issues to be considered are:
- What is the institutional policy? Purchase encouraged? Supported? Indifferent?
- Will computers be sold on campus? By the bookstore? By local dealers?

- Who will provide support (consulting, maintenance, and so on)?
- What is the role of a campus network?
- What support is there for curriculum change?
- What is the appropriate organization and budgeting process as more of the services become decentralized?

While some administrators assumed that purchase by students and faculty of personal computers would lower capital and operating fund needs for computing, the results are just the opposite. A rule of thumb for computer costs is to assume that the support and software costs will equal the hardware costs. Few institutions have been prepared for the increased operating budgets brought about by the capital expenditures for personal computers. Many computer centers have also added new functions, such as the support of personal computers, without new sources of funds.

Communications and Networks. Several forces have hastened the campus-wide planning of communications networks. One of the most important was the split of AT&T, which has caused examination of new alternatives to telephone systems. However, the replacement of current telephone systems is coinciding with the development of campus-wide networks that have emerged from timesharing facilities and distributed terminals (which are now being replaced by personal computers and departmental service minicomputers). Thus planning that had previously been independent is now linked, as some alternatives for overlap of the services emerge.

What Are the Objectives for the Evaluation?

The key question for any evaluation is, Compared to what? Are the computing services going to be compared with Carnegie-Mellon or MIT? Is it going to be compared to its peers? Do any plans exist so that its performance can be compared to them? Are the amount of resources it was promised when plans were developed known, so the constraints can be considered in evaluation?

Before an evaluation can start, the academic administrators need to reflect on the setting for the evaluation of computing services. They should determine whether they want to evaluate academic or administrative computing services (which may be provided through a single organizational unit). They should determine which framework of objectives, resources, and constraints should be used to set the stage. Have they ever explicitly linked computing services to university goals? How is the support for computing services distributed through the schools and departments? Who is accountable for computing in schools and departments? What are the responsibilities of the Academic/Administrative Computing Center for the operations of the equipment? Maintenance and support of campus networks? Support of software on mainframes and micros? Performing campus-wide planning and budgeting for computing? Dealing with computer vendors for acquisitions and maintenance? Reviewing and aiding proposed acquisitions of equipment by departments? Supporting faculty members in the development of software in support of the curriculum? Identifying and supporting data bases? Supporting connections to national networks?

A crucial element of the evaluation is to determine its scope and objectives. Which computing services will be evaluated? Who is responsible for them? Are there objectives and plans to measure against resources and constraints? Because the use of computers is widely distributed over the campus and reflects services that are not easily measured (effective versus inappropriate consulting, choices of standards and campus directions), many computing services are rarely evaluated except by the campus auditors checking the details of business procedures. Will the deans be responsible for the evaluation of the services that may be located in their schools?

The advent of the personal computer has brought significant changes to many campuses, and the long-term shift of resources has gone back to the individuals, due to rapid changes in price and performance. Few campuses today have only one mainframe for academic computing. Most use mixtures of mainframes, minis, and micros with access to supercomputers through available national networks. Evaluation options have shifted from an easily measured analysis of the operation of and user satisfaction with a single mainframe, to the evaluation of a complex set of processes satisfying many different local objectives.

Thus the first step in the evaluation of computing should be directed toward determining what and who should be evaluated, what are they responsible for, and what objectives and constraints exist. Another important task is determining the peers of the institution. Which comparable institutions have embarked on similar computing strategies? Rather than looking for peers by comparing computer resources, identify peers in terms of academic objectives, similar resources, and size. Some of these questions are closely related to the factors that should be considered in the development of a strategic computing plan for an institution. Strategic plans for computing require the identification of academic goals before determining technology and services. Too often a campus plan is just an implementation schedule rather than an indication of the academic objectives that will be fulfilled and the alternative strategies to be considered.

Emery (1984), while reviewing the issues in building an information technology strategy for an institution, identifies the following as important elements:

- Cultural climate within the institution

- Cultural and financial constraints on computing
- Statement of the plan's aspiration level
- Organizational structure of computing activities
- Types of computing services to be provided
- Mechanisms for selecting hardware and software
- Design and management of a network
- Means to motivate change within the curriculum
- Use of computing in scholarly activities
- Strategy for dealing with distributed computing
- Security and privacy of data
- Time-phased implementation steps
- Time-phased cost projections
- Mechanism for budgeting and charging for computing.

These elements can be helpful in understanding both the issues that should be considered in developing a campus strategy and in recognizing peers that will be useful for comparison purposes.

What Are Components of an Evaluation Plan?

Scope and Objective. An approach to evaluation should start with a clear identification of the objective and scope of the evaluation. Is the objective to provide an operationally focused review based on the concern for effective delivery of computer services? Is the objective to examine the campus strategy toward key computing issues and to determine its approach versus that of its peers? Is the development of the promised administrative data-processing integrated data base late and overrunning the budget?

It is important to write a brief statement of scope and objectives for the evaluation regardless of the method chosen for its completion. The scope and objectives should answer these questions:

What Is the Scope of the Evaluation? Will it be focused on academic or administrative computing? If academic, will it focus only on the services provided by the academic center, or will it examine other computing services? Is it aimed at comparing the results to the plan, or will it focus on faculty and student needs and perceptions? Will it include communication issues? Will it base its review on data collected or by existing reports, or will it perform surveys and interviews? What time will be allotted to the evaluation?

What Is the Objective of the Evaluation? Is it to be an evaluation that focuses on the status of planning? Will it be a review of the operations of the computer facilities? Will it be focused on the budget and academic needs? Is it a quick review to determine critical issues? Is it to be an extensive review to develop strategic and organizational options?

What Results Are Expected from the Evaluation? Is the evaluation to be focused on an oral presentation to senior administrators? Is an extensive report needed? Should the recommendations be focused on organization? Technology?

Constraints. Following the development of the scope and objectives, the constraints that need to be considered in the evaluation should be identified.

When Should the Evaluation Start, and When Should It End? Is the evaluation linked to budget schedules? Other evaluations or committee reviews?

What Resources Are Available for the Evaluation? Will faculty or administrative committees take part? Will staff members be available for support? Meeting rooms? Will there be travel funds for visiting other institutions? Will there be funds for professional consultants? Will funds be available for honoraria? Will there be funds or resources for clerical help or interview aid?

Which Organizations Will Participate in the Evaluation? Will the focus be academic or administrative? What role will the deans and schools play? Which administrators will be involved? Who will be responsible for the evaluation? Who will be responsible for the implementation of recommendations?

What Information Will Be Available for the Evaluation? Will the budget and planning documents be available? Are computing service statistics available? Are survey results and other studies available?

Approach. Following the development of the scope and objectives and the review of constraints, the approach should be developed. The key elements in the evaluation will be developing the approach to data collection that fits the scope, objectives, and constraints; the analysis of the data; and the development of recommendations and implementation. At this point, the major approaches to evaluation should be discussed.

Self-Evaluation. In self-evaluation, the computer service organization performs an evaluation of the services itself. It can perform this by reviewing the services, assessing their quality or appropriateness, and comparing accomplishments to goals and budgets. Self-evaluation can be useful, but often is limited as an evaluation process. It could be used as a step prior to another review (much as in the accrediting process).

Self-evaluation can be an important part of the process for evaluating computing services if it is performed regularly. Many computer centers regularly survey users and write self-evaluations as part of their annual reports, in which they compare achievements to goals and objectives for the previous year. Self-evaluation might be chosen as the approach if a baseline were needed or if there were no major problems.

Campus Committee. In this evaluation approach, a campus committee is charged to perform a review of the center. After settling the criteria and scope for the review, the committee develops the evaluation

plan. Sometimes the committee visits comparable institutions to obtain a broader perspective on the evaluation. Campus committees can provide an effective evaluation process, but often are limited by familiar factors:
- Who has the interests and breadth of understanding to take part?
- How much time can be devoted to the committee review?
- How much staff support can be provided?
- Can the committee be objective about the services?

Of course, there may be other factors that would affect the choice of a campus committee—the need for a campus consensus prior to any major changes, the availability and interest by faculty members, and so on. Normally there are faculty committees that supervise computing service, and an evaluation report could contribute to their review.

Visiting Committee. In this case, a committee of experts from other higher educational institutions is chosen to visit the campus and review the center(s). Generally the team is furnished with reports and information prior to the visit, which is usually of a two- or three-day duration. The team completes its analysis at the institutions, usually providing an oral exit briefing of its findings. This is followed by a brief written report. Potential visiting committee members can be identified by faculty or staff. There are also two programs of interest. The Association for Computing Machinery (ACM) Special Interest Group on University and College Computing Services (SIGUCCS) peer review program (Frobish, 1986) provides reviewers at the cost of travel and expenses only. This involves a commitment for your computing services organization to participate in peer reviews at other institutions. The ACM SIGUCCS group is the professional organization that serves campuses and universities throughout the United States and Canada. EDUCOM is a consortium of universities and colleges concerned with computing and networking issues and has a consulting arm with members drawn from higher education. EDUCOM can develop visiting evaluation committees that have the appropriate experience to aid in the review.

Generally, visiting committees are most effective when used to identify major issues and to provide an objective view of the issues. Since they are not usually able to spend significant amounts of time on the data collection and reviews, they will not be able to provide detailed implementation plans or extensive analysis.

Professional Consultants. There are a variety of firms that offer professional consulting services in computing and higher education. Consultants range in expertise from concentration on administrative data processing to expertise in telecommunications, academic administration, and academic computing. They can be provided through the consulting arms of the major accounting firms or by smaller firms formed by those experienced in higher education. The advantage of using consultants is their professionalism, their ability to devote sufficient time to the evaluation, and the opportunity for continuity (they are familiar with an institution and its issues and possess wide experience with the evaluation process). The disadvantage can be the cost and the difficulty in finding consultants with the appropriate experience (academic, administrative, academic administration).

Each of these approaches assumes a careful definition of the charges to the evaluation team and reasonable expectations about the quality and depth of reports or recommendations. The choices will depend on time, funds available for the evaluation, and the importance of issues. However, once the direction is made, the steps still will require attention and time.

Evaluation Design. Following the developing of the evaluation scope and objectives, the planning for the evaluation must resolve other important questions: To whom is the review team reporting? Who will provide staff help? What is the form of their report? The steps and tasks involved include preparation, visits, and reports.

Preparation should include a brief description of the current situation and major issues, identification of comparable or peer institutions, planning for timing on visits to the campus by the review team and to other campuses, development of survey or interview questions, selecting people to be interviewed, development of the interview schedule, collection of data and materials for the review team, and an interview or team room and support facilities. Visits may be done as briefings, interviews and visits to sites, informal assessments, development of an outline for the draft report, and exit interviews with the person responsible for the evaluation, committees, and computing service organizations. There are several reports prepared during the evaluation process. First, a draft report, then a preliminary review, a review for factual errors and omissions, the final report, and follow-up visits and reviews.

What Are Some Criteria for Evaluation?

Since the nature of computing services varies widely according to campus objectives and needs (computing at a research institution will have a different emphasis than at a liberal arts institution), the criteria will be general but will provide some key elements. Accreditation reviews often focus on four major areas (Accrediting Commission . . ., 1982): (1) What are the computing services, and how well are they supporting faculty and students in meeting their academic goals? (2) How effective is access to the services? (3) Are the number and quality of the staff appropriate? (4) Do the facilities match the needs?

The following questions help analyze and evaluate those broad criteria:

1. Is there a written institutional plan for computing?
2. Are there annual reports for computing services?
3. Is computing an element in the planning and budgeting process for each school or department?
4. How effective is the planning linkage between the computing plans and the institutional plans and budget?
5. Does the variety of computing services (hardware, software, professional support staff, network access to national resources such as data bases or supercomputers) match the campus needs for computing?
6. What is the number of public terminals or personal computers per student?
7. What is the number of personal computers or terminals per faculty member?
8. What is the total number of public terminals available?
9. How convenient is access to computing services? Hours available? Hours of consulting?
10. What support services (consulting, documentation, software, hardware selection) are available, and at what level are they provided?
11. Do the data and communications services ensure privacy of records and data?
12. Are there adequate records of major computer service?
13. Are there effective feedback mechanisms (newsletters, faculty and user committees, published plans, surveys) for communication with the users?
14. Are there standards or guidelines published for connection to the network or services?

How Are the Results Implemented?

One issue that needs to be considered is the implementation of recommendations. How will they be reviewed? Who will determine if the recommendations are appropriate? Who will be responsible for seeing that they are carried out? Who will track their implementation? Who will "own" the recommendations? The academic administrator to whom it reports? A faculty committee? It is too easy for a list of recommendations from an evaluation committee to be ignored, when no one was charged with their implementation.

Conclusion

The process of evaluating computing services can be a straightforward activity if the approach follows the structure used for other evaluations and technology is not used to obfuscate the academic issues that should drive the activity. This will require discipline and may involve steps that may not have already been accomplished—particularly framing the goals and objectives for computing within the institutional setting. Still, evaluation can be effective and will aid in ensuring that the goals and services for computing are in harmony with the institution's goals.

References

Accrediting Commission for Senior Colleges and Universities. *Handbook of Accreditation.* Oakland, Calif.: Western Association of Schools and Colleges, 1982.

Emery, J. C. "Issues in Building an Information Technology Strategy." *EDUCOM Bulletin,* 1984, *19* (3), 4–13.

Frobish, M. (ed.). *PEER REVIEW: A Program to Improve Computing Services in Higher Education.* Research Triangle Park, N.C.: Association for Computing Machinery, Special Interest Group on University and College Computing Services, 1986.

Gillespie, R. G. "How Computers Are Transforming Higher Education." In P. J. Tate and M. Kressel (eds.), *The Expanding Role of Telecommunications in Higher Education.* New Directions for Higher Education, no. 44. San Francisco: Jossey-Bass, 1983.

Levine, L., Strenta, C., and Wolford, G. *The Impact of the Macintosh at Dartmouth (1984/1985).* Hanover, N.H.: The MacCommittee, Dartmouth University, 1986.

Warlick, C. H. (ed.). *1986 Directory of Computing Facilities in Higher Education,* Austin: University of Texas at Austin Computation Center with Seminars for Academic Computing, 1986.

Robert G. Gillespie is a principal in the higher education computing, planning, and consulting firm of Gillespie, Folkner and Associates, Inc. He has served as vice provost for computing of the University of Washington and as chair of the subcommittee on computing for the Accrediting Commission for Senior Colleges and Universities, Western Association of Schools and Colleges.

A synthesis of the contributed chapters suggests a need for an eclectic approach to evaluation design and a greater emphasis on internal monitoring and use of results.

Evaluating Administrative Services and Programs: Making the Process More Useful

Jon F. Wergin, Larry A. Braskamp

After reading all of the ideas and strategies described in the preceding chapters, a campus administrator may wonder whether evaluation is worth all the trouble. Given the variety of potential targets for a formal evaluation effort and the prospect of the bureaucratic tangle that might result, the initial response might well be, "Why bother?" Institutions periodically have to undergo accreditation self-studies anyway, and the interval between them is sufficiently short that administrators are either planning for one, going through one, reacting to the consequences, or, at the very least, have fresh memories of what the experience was like. In addition, much of what has passed for formal review in the past has been ritualistic: go through the motions, please the evaluators, and then return to business as usual. In many places the regard for evaluation by both administrators and the campus officers involved is guarded at best, hostile at worst.

Authors of the preceding chapters have all taken a different view, arguing that evaluation is important, timely, and in the best interests of the institution. External demands abound, whether they are headline-grabbing athletic scandals, or more prosaic calls for greater efficiency in business affairs. William Bennett's now-famous attack on the complacency, mismanagement—even greed—in higher education (1986) demands attention, if not acquiescence. And as some of the contributors to this sourcebook have noted, serious evaluation is essential for self-improvements and better service to the institution and its students.

This final chapter addresses the problem and opportunity of evaluation directly from the perspective of the campus administrator or institutional researcher. We will start by suggesting criteria for deciding whether formal evaluation is worthwhile, then discuss several considerations for designing evaluation strategies, based in large measure on the insights presented by the contributing authors; and finally suggest how evaluation may enhance organizational health and effectiveness.

The Value of Evaluation

In deciding whether formal evaluation is worthwhile, several criteria are paramount. All relate to the concept of utilization. Patton (1978) has perhaps defined it best: "Utilization occurs when there is an immediate, concrete, and observable effect on specific decisions and program activities resulting directly from evaluation findings" (p. 24). Studies on utilizing evaluative information, by Patton and others (1977) and Braskamp and Brown (1980), among others, have shown consistently that the prospects for genuine impact of evaluation depend on the presence and strength of several factors:

1. Identification of specific individuals or groups who have an interest in the evaluation being done and the information it generates. The key word here is *specific*—not a diffuse and anonymous label like "the faculty" or "the federal government," but a clear definition of the users, their interests, and their needs.

2. A clear and unambiguous focus. What are the purposes for undertaking the evaluation? What questions are to be answered? What is to be done with the information? In short, how relevant will the evaluation be to the users defined above? As Patton (1978) has correctly pointed out, little is to be gained by conducting an evaluation that will provide information that people know already or do not care about.

3. A shared understanding of how the data are to be interpreted and used. Evaluations will probably not have much impact when questions about the meaning of the data collected are deferred until after the fact. It is better to raise questions like the following in advance: "What would we do if we found that . . .," or "What difference will this information make?" Not to ask these questions is to risk collecting information that is not only useless but vulnerable to political manipulation and distortion.

A related question is to consider whether resources are available for improvement. Organizational and program diagnosis without any thought of possible intervention strategies to be taken is dangerous and ultimately dysfunctional. Discovering widespread faculty dissatisfaction with consulting services provided by the academic computing office will not itself lead to positive change; appropriate intervention strategies require a commitment of resources needed to solve the problem—more staff, better training, more accessible facilities, and so on—and top administrative commitment to the evaluation process.

Considerations for Design

Once the decision has been made to pursue a formal evaluation, numerous design considerations must be taken into account. The previous authors have all mentioned some; we believe that three are most important: (1) understanding the context of the program, (2) determining the appropriate emphases, and (3) deciding how comprehensive the evaluation should be.

Program Context. Perhaps the strongest impression gained from perusing the previous chapters is the importance of understanding how an administrative unit fits within the institution—not just its functions and goals, but also its character, culture, modes of operation, and unique problems. Davis, for example, has suggested that a concern unique to the athletic program of a campus is the balance between competitiveness and academic performance, the problem of how to maintain and enhance athletic visibility without exploiting student athletes. Brown has discussed how counseling centers face constant pressure to establish an appropriate relative emphasis on preventive, remedial, and developmental services, while struggling with traditional stereotypes of counseling centers. Seagren and Miller have pointed out that business affairs offices must continually weigh the competitive advantage of campus-run enterprises with those available in the private sector. A single evaluation model or approach to data collection will not work well with such diversity, just as one method of evaluating teaching effectiveness will not work well for different kinds of courses, students, and teaching styles. The evaluation must be responsive to various program contexts and concerns, as Stake (1975) pointed out years ago. The key is close collaboration with program staff and a commitment to incorporating their perspectives.

Emphasis. Based upon the nature of the evaluation question and unique program concerns and contexts, a range of decisions will be implied. These may be categorized as effectiveness versus efficiency decisions, and formative versus summative decisions.

The effectiveness-efficiency distinction refers to the type of decisions to be made. An emphasis on program effectiveness implies a need to demonstrate the institutional worth of the program or of one or more of its components. Such a focus is likely to be important when a program or activity is experimental or when its purpose or goals are questioned. In this volume, Young has built a strong argument that the appropriate focus for evaluation of faculty development programs is the assessment of program goals; Sedlacek has shown that the appropriate focus for student academic support services is assessment of student outcomes. An emphasis on efficiency, in contrast, reflects a need to optimize allocation of resources. This focus is appropriate when the unit and its goals are well-established, and concerns center around potential cost-saving measures. A clear example is the bottom line emphasis of Seagren and Miller's chapter on business affairs, or the management emphasis of Gillespie's chapter on computing offices.

The formative-summative distinction refers to how the data are to be used. A formative evaluation is primarily concerned with program improvement, while a summative evaluation is mostly concerned with overall judgments of worth. These contrasting purposes require different kinds of data. A formative evaluation tends to be served best by routine reports, or an ongoing monitoring system; both require substantial investment by internal program staff. A summative evaluation, on the other hand, may require the services of a campus ad hoc committee, or the commissioning of a special study. Shirley, in his discussion of academic planning, illustrates this distinction nicely by illustrating cases that require formative versus summative approaches.

Of course, the effectiveness/efficiency and formative/summative dimensions are not dichotomous. Most evaluations will have all four elements, and the relative emphases will be a matter of degree. The appropriate emphasis will depend on the nature of the evaluation questions to be addressed. Consider the matrix in Figure 1. The sample evaluation questions represent four combinations of emphasis. A formative/effectiveness study concentrates on improving outcomes, a formative/efficiency study focuses on shifting resources among activities, a summative/effectiveness study concentrates on continuing versus terminating an activity based on demonstrated impact, and a summative/efficiency study

Figure 1. Types of Evaluation Questions

	Effectiveness	*Efficiency*
Formative	How congruent is strategic planning to the institutional mission?	Are computing resources being optimally used?
Summative	Should an internal faculty exchange program continue?	Should the institution get out of the bookstore business?

emphasizes continuation decisions based on return on investment. Each type calls for a different study design. In the first example, the appropriate approach might be an internal content analysis of planning documents for logical relationships, and an analysis of organizational planning responsibilities. In the second, the best strategy might be to compare service utilization and staff time-on-task data, with identified institutional priorities. In the third, faculty interest and participation in the activity could be weighed against alternative faculty development strategies. And in the fourth, a cost analysis is needed.

Comprehensiveness. The key issue here is one of evaluation cost. Wilson's description in Chapter One of a hierarchy of approaches is useful in this regard. A desk audit, at one extreme, is low in cost and obtrusiveness, but suffers from a lack of multiple perspectives. A comprehensive study, at the other extreme, has opposite characteristics. The optimal investment depends upon the economic and political consequences of the decision to be made. An evaluation question that involves relatively small costs (both direct and opportunity costs), or that will involve relatively small adjustments in power relationships, is most efficiently done with an informal desk audit approach, thus saving more comprehensive studies for larger questions, or those raised by the desk audit itself. Evaluations should ultimately be cost-free: the return should equal the investment.

Conclusion

Several important commonalities may be gleaned from the preceding chapters. These are general enough to apply to virtually any program, whether covered in this volume or not. First is the centrality of user satisfaction as a criterion not only in such obvious contexts as faculty development and student academic support but also in such diverse settings as athletics, planning, and business affairs. The ultimate consumer of the program or service must first be identified and their needs determined. Second is the importance of multiple perspectives and methods in the evaluation design. Focusing publicly on only one or a few indices of effectiveness tends to cheapen their value as criteria. For example, if a college admissions office were evaluated solely on average SAT scores of entering freshmen or numbers of applications, these measures would likely become surrogate objectives. They may be useful as part of a larger portrayal, but become dangerous when taken out of context. Third is the importance of unit involvement. Externally imposed evaluations without consultation and negotiation with program staff not only violate the organizational context, they also invite hostility, resentment, and even sabotage. Without genuine investment in the process by those who have the most to gain or lose, improvement is unlikely.

The ultimate goal of all evaluation is, after all, organizational improvement. Periodically singling out one campus office or another for the evaluation spotlight can be a myopic and ritualistic exercise. Evaluation works best when it becomes an integral part of the institution's way of doing things. The most important role for evaluation is to help the institution know itself better—to uncover its diverse strengths and nurture them, to disclose its weaknesses and improve them, and to do both under the umbrella of the institutional mission. Bennis (1984) has introduced a concept he calls "organizational learning," which he describes as "the capacity to find ways and means through which the organization can monitor its own performance, compare results with established objectives, have access to a continuously evolving data base on which to review past actions and base future ones, and how, if necessary, the organizational structure and key personnnel must be abandoned or rearranged when faced with new conditions" (p. 66). In our view, three conditions must exist for organizational learning to occur in higher education.

First and foremost is the climate set by the institution's top administration. Accountability is important, but not the sort of "accountability for results" that stifles creativity and punishes risk taking. More appropriate and constructive is "accountability for evaluation"—an institutional mandate to administrative units and progams to continually define their priorities and assess their performance in light of the institution's mission.

Second is a decentralized approach to evaluation, a perspective that evaluation is not something that is done to a unit. One implication of this approach is greater unit responsibility for use of evaluation data. Another is a shift in focus, away from ad hoc evaluations and toward more routine internal monitoring. Finally, a decentralized approach provides more flexibility for the development and testing of alternative program strategies: new ways of looking at faculty development, for example, or strategic planning.

A final necessary condition is the attitude toward evaluation itself. Receiving feedback on one's performance can be inhibiting or motivating; it can lead to temporary improvement to meet some external demand or standard, or it can lead to increased motivation to improve. The latter will occur more frequently in an institution characterized by an administration that is supportive of its people, yet serious about giving them feedback; by a management philosophy that decentralizes control over information and autonomy for making changes; and finally by an atmosphere of commitment to common goals.

In short, effective evaluation is not an adjunct to normal administrative functioning; it is central both in spirit and in practice to the operation of the unit. Evaluation focuses discussion on major issues, draws attention to the role of the office within the institution, and forces attention to important priorities. The ultimate goal of evaluation is to be part of an organization's conscious and deliberate pursuit of excellence.

References

Bennett, W. J. "Speech Delivered to Harvard University." *Chronicle of Higher Education*, October 15, 1986, pp. 27-30.
Bennis, W. "Transformative Power and Leadership." In T. S. Sergiovanni and J. E. Corbally (eds.), *Leadership and Organizational Culture*. Urbana: University of Illinois Press, 1984.
Braskamp, L. A., and Brown, R. D. (eds.). *Utilization of Evaluative Information*. New Directions for Program Evaluation, no. 5. San Francisco: Jossey-Bass, 1980.
Patton, M. Q. *Utilization-Focused Evaluation*. Newbury Park, Calif.: Sage, 1978.
Patton, M. Q., Grimes, P. S., Guthrie, K. M., Brennan, N. J., French, B. D., and Blyth, D. A. "In Search of Impact: An Analysis of the Utilization of Federal Health Evaluation Research." In C. Weiss (ed.), *Using Social Research in Public Policy Making*. Lexington, Mass.: Lexington Books, 1977.
Stake, R. E. (ed.). *Evaluating the Arts in Education: A Responsive Approach*. Westerville, Ohio: Merrill, 1975.

Jon F. Wergin is associate director of the Center for Educational Development and Faculty Resources at Virginia Commonwealth University in Richmond.

Larry A. Braskamp is director of instructional and management services at the University of Illinois, Urbana-Champaign.

Index

A

Academic affairs, business affairs related to, 27
Accrediting Commission for Senior Colleges and Universities, 90, 92
Activity: evaluation of, for counseling centers, 62-65, 69; outcomes of, 63-65; profile of, 62-63
Ad hoc/special studies, for business affairs, 31-35
Allen, T. R., 63, 70
Ansoff, H. I., 16, 23
Arbona, C., 52, 56
Archibald, S. O., 29, 36
Association for Computing Machinery (ACM), Special Interest Group on University and College Computing Services (SIGUCCS) of, 89
Association of American Colleges, 1, 2, 72, 81
Athletics programs: administration of, 42-43; analysis of evaluating, 37-47; background on, 37; barriers to evaluating, 38; checklist for, 39-40; and compliance with rules, 45-46; conclusion on, 46; control of, 41-43; financing of, 42; and institutional philosophy and culture, 40-41; student services and resources in, 43-45

B

Balance: in athletics programs, 41; of goals, 61
Banning, J., 62, 69
Barak, R. J., 4, 5, 12
Becker, S. L., 42, 46
Bennett, W. J., 1, 2, 94, 99
Bennis, W., 98, 99
Bereiter, C., 52, 56
Berg, N. A., 16, 23
Blue-ribbon committees, for business affairs, 32-33
Blyth, D. A., 99

Board of Higher Education (Illinois), 4, 8, 12
Bok, D., 38, 41, 43-44, 46
Boyer, E., 1, 2, 72, 82
Boyer, S. P., 52, 56
Bradburn, N. M., 55, 57
Braskamp, L. A., 2, 93, 94, 99
Braun, S., 11, 12
Brennan, N. J., 99
Brooks, G. C., Jr., 52, 55
Brown, R. D., 59, 60, 66, 69-70, 94, 95, 99
Brown, W. B., 19, 23
Burks, D. R., 7, 12
Bush Foundation, 71-72
Business affairs: academic affairs related to, 27; ad hoc/special studies for, 31-35; analysis of evaluating, 25-36; and availability of services, 29-30; clients of, 28, 29; context of, 26-28; criteria for, 28-30; data collection and interpretation for, 30-35; defined, 25-26; and financial considerations, 29; organization of, 26; organizational issues for, 27-28; summary on, 35; user satisfaction with, 29

C

Calgary, University of, complex plan at, 11
California, University of, complex plan of, 7, 11
Carnegie Foundation for the Advancement of Teaching, 1
Chaffee, E. E., 27, 35
Chief business officer, purposes of, 26
Choi, H. C., 42, 46
Christensen, C. R., 16, 23
Clients: of business affairs, 28, 29; and nonclients of counseling centers, 66
Colonial League, 41
Community service, evaluating, 54
Comprehensive review, model of, 11
Computing services: academic and

101

Computing Services *(continued)*
administrative functions of, 83-84; analysis of evaluating, 83-92; background on, 83-84; and communications and networks, 85; components in evaluating, 87-90; conclusion on, 91-92; constraints on, 88; cost of, 84; criteria for, 90-91; evaluation design for, 90; and implementation, 91; issues of, 84-85; objectives for evaluating, 85-88; and personal computers, 84-85, 86

Connoisseurship evaluation, model of, 5

Conrad, C. F., 5, 12

Consultants: for business affairs, 31-32; for computing services, 89-90; and planning, 21-22

Corazzini, J. G., 61, 70

Cost-benefit analysis, 67-68

Cost-effectiveness analysis, 67

Counseling centers: activity evaluation for, 62-65, 69; analysis of evaluating, 59-70; background on, 59-60; clients and nonclients of, 66; conclusion on, 68-69; cost-outcome analysis of, 66-68; goal evaluation for, 60-62, 69; impact evaluation for, 65-68, 69; and institutional climate, 66; role perceptions and expectations in, 64; user satisfaction with, 65-66

Cunningham, R. L., 44, 46

D

Data: for business affairs, 30-35; gathering, for faculty development programs, 77-79; integration of, 80-81; for planning, 18-19

Davis, B. G., 37, 39, 46, 47, 95

Day, J. D., 51, 56

Decision-oriented evaluation: for faculty development programs, 77; model of, 5; and planning, 16-18

Desk review, model of, 9-10

Drucker, P. F., 1, 2

E

Easton, A., 27, 35

Eble, K. E., 71, 72, 73, 82

EDUCOM, 89

Eisner, E. W., 5, 12

Eitzen, D. S., 43, 45, 46

Emery, J. C., 86, 92

Entwisle, D. R., 50, 56

Erickson, G., 71, 82

Evaluation: of administrative units, 3-13, 93-99; of athletics programs, 37-47; barriers to, 3-4, 38; of business affairs, 25-36; commonalities in, 97-99; comprehensiveness of, 97; of computing service, 83-92; considerations in, 7-8; context of, 4-5, 95; of counseling centers, 59-70; design considerations for, 77-81, 90, 95-97; effectiveness-efficiency focus of, 95-96; emphasis of, 95-97; of faculty development programs, 71-82; formative-summative focus of, 96; framework for, 8-11; goals of, 98, 99; impact of, 11-12; interest in, 4; need for, 93-94; of planning, 15-23; principles of, 6, 50; process of, 5-6, 93-99; purposes of, 5; steps in, 5; of student support services, 49-57; utilization of, 94; value of, 94-95

F

Faculty: counseling center contacts with, 64; as internal experts, and business affairs, 34-35

Faculty development programs: analysis of evaluating goals of, 71-82; audience for evaluation of, 76; background on, 71-73; conclusion on, 81; design of evaluating, 77-81; goals and objectives of, 74-75; goals evaluation for, 73-76; reasons for evaluating, 73-76

Fairness, need for, 6

Foley, W. J., 12, 57

Ford Foundation, 72

Fort Union State University, faculty development goals at, 75

Freeman, H. E., 50, 57

French, B. D., 99

Frobish, M., 89, 92

G

Gaff, J. G., 72, 82

Gephart, W. J., 12, 57

Gillespie, R. G., 83, 84, 92, 96
Gilley, J. W., 38, 41, 42, 46
Goal, activity, and impact (GAI) evaluation, and counseling centers, 59-60, 68-69
Goal-based evaluation, model of, 5
Goals: balance of, 61; evaluation of, 60-62, 69, 73-76; of faculty development programs, 71-82; long-range, 53; and resources, 61-62; worth of, 60-61
Gore, F. J., 31, 35
Governing board, and planning, 20-21
Greiner, J. M., 51, 56
Griffin, G., 7, 12
Grimes, P. S., 99
Guba, E. G., 12, 57
Guth, W. D., 32, 35
Guthrie, K. M., 99

H

Hammond, R. L., 12, 57
Hanford, G. H., 37, 42, 46
Hickey, A., 38, 41, 42, 46
Higher education: nature of, and business affairs, 26-27; organizational learning in, 88
Hufnagel, R., 43, 45, 46
Humphrey, L. L., 51, 55, 56
Humphreys, S., 39, 46
Hunger, J. D., 16, 23
Hurley, R. B., 44, 46
Hurst, J. C., 60, 62, 70

I

Illinois, evaluation required in, 4, 8, 12
Illinois at Urbana-Champaign, University of, evaluation at, 8-12
Impact evaluation, for counseling centers, 65-68, 69
Institutional planning. *See* Planning
Institutions, culture of, 40-41, 66
Integrity, in athletics programs, 40-41
Intercollegiate athletics programs. *See* Athletics programs
Internal audits, for business affairs, 32
Internal review committee: for business affairs, 33; for computing service, 88-89

Isaac, S., 50, 55, 56
Ivy League, 41

J

Johnson, J. R., 33, 35
Johnston, P. H., 51, 56
Jones, D. P., 31, 36

K

Karoly, P., 51, 56
Key Evaluation Checklist, 39
Kirschenbaum, D. S., 51, 55, 56
Knowledge, evaluating acquisition of, 54
Kuh, G. D., 50, 56

L

Lateral review, model of, 10-11
Leadership, evaluating, 54
Lederman, D., 41, 46
Lelong, D., 16, 23
Levin, H., 67, 70
Levine, L., 84, 92
Lilly Endowment, 72

M

McCorkle, C. O., Jr., 29, 36
McKeachie, W. J., 71, 72, 73, 82
McManus, J. B., 8, 12
Malett, S. D., 51, 55, 56
Marcus, L. R., 33, 35
Merriman, R. L., 12, 57
Michael, W. B., 50, 55, 56
Mihalich, J. C., 41, 46
Miller, G. A., 25, 36, 95, 96
Moberg, A. J., 19, 23
Morrill, W. H., 60, 62, 70
Myers, R. C., 43, 47

N

National Collegiate Athletic Association (NCAA), 39-40, 43, 45, 46
National Endowment for the Humanities, 1
National Institute of Education, 1, 2, 72, 82
National Science Foundation, 84

Noncognitive questionnaire (NCQ), for student support services, 52
North, University of the, faculty development program at, 73-81

O

Oetting, E. R., 60, 62, 70
Operational reports, in business affairs, 30-31
Organizational learning, factors in, 98

P

Palinscar, A. S., 51, 56
Paris, S. G., 51, 56
Passive failure, in reading, 51
Patton, M. Q., 94, 99
Pauk, W., 51, 56
Pembina College, faculty development goals at, 75
Perri, M. G., 51, 56, 57
Planning: analysis of evaluating, 15-23; data for, 18-19; decisional aspects of, 16-18; defined, 15-16; methods of evaluating, 22; operational, 16; process for, 19-20; roles in evaluating, 20-22; strategic, 16; summary on, 22-23
Planning council, role of, 21, 22, 23
Planning support staff, role of, 21, 22, 23
Porto, B. L., 43, 46
President, and planning, 21, 22
Provus, M. M., 12, 57
Purdy, D. A., 43, 45, 46

R

Racism, evaluating understanding of, 53
Reading, evaluating program for, 51-52
Resources, and goals, 61-62
Responsive evaluation, model of, 5
Responsiveness, need for, 6
Rhatigan, J. J., 43, 47
Richards, C. S., 51, 57
Robinson, F., 51, 57
Rossi, P. H., 50, 57

S

Salter, M. S., 16, 23
Scardamalia, M., 52, 56
Scott, R. A., 1, 2
Scriven, M., 39, 46, 47, 61, 70, 71, 82
Seagren, A. T., 25, 36, 95, 96
Sedgwick, K., 32, 36
Sedlacek, W. E., 49, 52, 55, 56, 57, 96
Self-appraisal, evaluating, 53
Self-concept, evaluating, 52-53
Self-evaluation, by computing services, 88
Sell, L., 42, 46
Shapiro, J. Z., 38, 47
Shirley, R. C., 15, 16, 23, 96
Sparks, W. G., 42, 46
Stake, R. E., 5, 12, 95, 99
Stonewater, B. B., 63, 70
Stonewater, J. K., 63, 70
Strategic review, model of, 10
Strenta, C., 84, 92
Strickland, A. J., III, 19, 23
Student support services: analysis of evaluating, 49-57; in athletics programs, 43-45; background on, 49-50; conclusion on, 55-56; defined, 49; implementing evaluation of, 54-55; intervention strategies of, 55; measures of, 55; nontraditional variables in, 52-54; program objectives for, 54-55; traditional variables in, 50-52
Students, counseling center contacts with, 64
Study skills, evaluating program for, 50-51
Stufflebeam, D. L., 5, 12, 50, 57
Sudman, S., 55, 57
Sullivan, L. L., 71, 82
Support person, evaluating use of, 53-54

T

Thomas, S., 39, 46
Thompson, A. A., Jr., 19, 23
Thompson, M., 67, 70
Timeliness: need for, 6; of planning, 17-18
Todd, R. K., 8, 12

Tracey, T. J., 52, 55, 57
Tyler, R. W., 5, 12

U

User satisfaction: with business affairs, 29; centrality of, 97; with counseling centers, 65–66
Utilization, factors for, 94

V

Visiting committee, for computer services, 89

W

Warlick, C. H., 84, 92
Welzenbach, L. F., 25–27, 36
Wergin, J. F., 2, 72, 73, 80, 82, 93, 99
Wheatland University, faculty development goals at, 75
Wheelen, T. L., 16, 23
White, T. J., 52, 57
Whitner, P. A., 43, 47
Wilson, R. F., 1, 3, 5, 8, 12, 13, 97
Winograd, P. N., 51, 56
Wixson, K. K., 51, 56
Wolford, G., 84, 92
Wright, R. G., 31, 35
Wright, S. R., 50, 57
Writing, evaluating programs in, 52

Y

Young, R. E., 71, 82, 96

STATEMENT OF OWNERSHIP, MANAGEMENT AND CIRCULATION

1. TITLE OF PUBLICATION: New Directions for Institutional Research
A. PUBLICATION NO.: 0 9 8 - 8 3 0
2. DATE OF FILING: 10/7/87
3. FREQUENCY OF ISSUE: quarterly
4. NO. OF ISSUES PUBLISHED ANNUALLY: 4
5. ANNUAL SUBSCRIPTION PRICE: $36 indiv/$48 inst

4. COMPLETE MAILING ADDRESS OF KNOWN OFFICE OF PUBLICATION: 433 California St., San Francisco, San Francisco County, CA 94104

5. COMPLETE MAILING ADDRESS OF THE HEADQUARTERS OR GENERAL BUSINESS OFFICES OF THE PUBLISHERS: 433 California St., San Francisco, San Francisco County, CA 94104

6. FULL NAMES AND COMPLETE MAILING ADDRESS OF PUBLISHER, EDITOR, AND MANAGING EDITOR

PUBLISHER: Jossey-Bass Inc., Publishers, 433 California St., San Francisco CA 94104

EDITOR: Patrick T. Terenzini, Institute of Higher Education, Candler Hall, University of Georgia, Athens, GA 30602

MANAGING EDITOR: Allen Jossey-Bass, Jossey-Bass Publishers, 433 California St., SF CA 94104

7. OWNER

FULL NAME	COMPLETE MAILING ADDRESS
Jossey-Bass Inc., Publishers	433 California St., SF CA 94104
for names and addresses of stockholders, see attached list	

8. KNOWN BONDHOLDERS, MORTGAGEES, AND OTHER SECURITY HOLDERS OWNING OR HOLDING 1 PERCENT OR MORE OF TOTAL AMOUNT OF BONDS, MORTGAGES OR OTHER SECURITIES

FULL NAME	COMPLETE MAILING ADDRESS
same as #7	

10. EXTENT AND NATURE OF CIRCULATION

	AVERAGE NO. COPIES EACH ISSUE DURING PRECEDING 12 MONTHS	ACTUAL NO. COPIES OF SINGLE ISSUE PUBLISHED NEAREST TO FILING DATE
A. TOTAL NO. COPIES (Net Press Run)	1900	2036
B. PAID CIRCULATION		
1. Sales through dealers and carriers, street vendors and counter sales	231	93
2. Mail Subscription	977	980
C. TOTAL PAID CIRCULATION	1208	1073
D. FREE DISTRIBUTION BY MAIL, CARRIER OR OTHER MEANS, SAMPLES, COMPLIMENTARY AND OTHER FREE COPIES	70	213
E. TOTAL DISTRIBUTION	1278	1286
F. COPIES NOT DISTRIBUTED		
1. Office use, left over, unaccounted, spoiled after printing	622	750
2. Return from news agents		
G. TOTAL	1900	2036

11. I certify that the statements made by me above are correct and complete

Vice-President